RED PAINT

Red Paint

THE ANCESTRAL AUTOBIOGRAPHY
OF A COAST SALISH PUNK

Sasha taqʷšəblu LaPointe

COUNTERPOINT

Berkeley, California

Red Paint

Library of Congress Cataloging-in-Publication Data
Names: LaPointe, Sasha taqwšeblu, author.
Title: Red paint : the ancestral autobiography of a Coast Salish
punk / Sasha taqwšeblu LaPointe.
Description: First hardcover edition. | Berkeley, California :
Counterpoint Press, 2022. | Author's name is spelled: Sasha
taqwš[schwa]blu, the "e" in her Coast Salish name in all instances
the "e" should be a schwa, an upside down e and the "w" is written
in superscript. —Publisher's email.
Identifiers: LCCN 2021029010 | ISBN 9781640094147 (hardcover) |
ISBN 9781640094154 (ebook)
Subjects: LCSH: LaPointe, Sasha taqwšeblu. | Coast Salish
Indians—Washington (State)—Biography. | Salishan women—
Washington State)—Biography. | Coast Salish Indians—History. |
Coast Salish Indians—Social life and customs. | Punk culture—
Washington (State) | Psychic trauma—Washington (State) |
Resilience (Personality trait)—Washington (State)
Classification: LCC E99.S21 L36 2022 | DDC 979.7004/97940092
[B]—dc23
LC record available at https://lccn.loc.gov/2021029010

Jacket design by Nicole Caputo
Book design by Jordan Koluch

COUNTERPOINT
2560 Ninth Street, Suite 318
Berkeley, CA 94710
www.counterpointpress.com

Printed in the United States of America

1 3 5 7 9 10 8 6 4 2

For the women who came before me,
and for Violet

Red Paint

If you look at the cedar

ʔəbilʼ čəxʷ gʷəšuuc tiʔəʔ x̌payʼ

you'll see how it bends

č(ə)xʷa šudxʷ ʔəsčal kʷi suqəčil

and doesn't break

gʷəl xʷiʔ gʷəsuxʷəƛ̓

and you have to learn how to be like the cedar,

gʷəl yawʼ čəxʷ ləhaʔdxʷ ʔəsčal kʷ(i) adsəshuy
ʔəsʔistəʔ ʔə tiʔəʔ x̌pay

how to be flexible and pliable

ʔəsčal kʷi səsqʼəčil gʷəl ʔə(s)səpil

and you yourself will not break.

gʷəl xʷiʔ kʷi gʷ(ə)adsux̌ʷəƛ̓.

        —Violet taqʷšəblu Hilbert

(Translation requested by Sasha taqʷšəblu LaPointe

Translated by Zalmai ʔəswəli Zahir, March 11, 2020)

RED PAINT

From Aunt Susie's Salmon Song

Transcribed and translated by Violet taqʷšəblu Hilbert, from gʷəqʷulcəʔ/ *Aunt Susie Sampson Peter; the Wisdom of a Skagit Elder*

*I was sick, I was sick for a long
time. Spiritually, supernaturally
ill.
For the entire salmon season, during all of the
runs. We caught humpback salmon first.
We killed them. Indeed we killed them.*

*As a consequence, it seems the salmon took
me. They ran off with me (my soul).
There I was sick.*

I was medicated (treated) yet I became progressively
worse. It took place there on the Skagit River.
There I lay (for an indefinite time) until the salmon run
finished. I became very thin.
My stomach was
compressed. No food was
inside.
I was skinny.

When I would feel it, my face was only bone.

Then I dreamed! I dreamed! I overheard talking,

"Oh you folks had better return that human
woman. You should return her to her human
world.
You, the one called skʷaysəliwəʔ, will return her."
The leader with a great big canoe was thus
identified. Many other people were on board.
With their red paint

and cedar bark headdresses on.

I was traveling on the back of a
salmon. That is how I was canoed.
I was very afraid that I would fall off and drown.
Then I overheard in song:
Unload her now, skʷaysəliwəʔ,.

You have arrived back in your
land. You will disembark.
You will say to your own grandmother, "Open the door for
me. I came back."
I walked upland, I knocked on the door.
"Open the door, Grandmother. I have arrived."

But they said of me I was crazy (confused, they said).
Grandmother said,
"Get a grip on yourself, for you did not just
arrive, my dear little one,
you have instead always been
here, asleep continuously and
dreaming."

Prologue:
Winter Dances

We were a hunter-gatherer society. We were nomadic. We lived along the coasts and on the rivers. We moved with the water. We moved with the resources and followed the supply of fish. We picked berries and bracken root. We wove garments out of cedar, and mats for sleeping out of cattail grass. Shellfish and salmon were important to us. We lived in cedar plank houses. We lived communally.

And we held winter ceremonies. In the longhouse, people gathered. They built a great fire, they banished spirits in an opening ritual, and then they danced. They danced to the pounding of drums. On dirt floors, with bare feet, with smoke thick in the air, my ancestors danced until dawn broke.

When the missionaries arrived, they banned the Coast Salish peoples' spiritual practices.

So ceremonies went underground and for the first time were held in secret. Treaties were passed and eventually the Salish ancestral religion was given back to the people, but now it was something protected, something private.

It is not my job to tell the story of what happens in the longhouse. It would be considered disrespectful. My mother has taught me to behave a certain way, to honor and uphold our traditions and the wishes of my elders. We come from a long line of Salish medicine workers. We respect this. What happens in the longhouse is not what this story is about, but this is a story about healing. This is a story about what I've learned from my ancestors. My ancestors participated in the winter dances.

They wore red paint.

hədiw

There is a word that hangs next to the front door of my parents' home. Written on an index card in black ink it reads "hədiw." It is the Lushootseed word for "come in." It welcomes me. Every time I see the sign, I sound out the word and wonder if I am saying it wrong. *Hu-dee-ew.* I have never learned to speak our tribe's traditional language.

On a rainy afternoon in midsummer, I walked up the road to visit my parents. I had a question to ask. I came to the door, the word and I had our ritual, then I punched in the security code: 1-4-9-2. *Really, this is the code.* Sometimes it's easier to remember the hard things. The year Columbus "discovered" America clicked the mechanism unlocking the front door and letting me into my family's home. I've often wished I understood the technology well enough to program 1-4-9-1.

It is a small house. Small and old. And it has been in my family for generations. It sits on the large slope of a yard, on a hill that looks out toward Mount Tahoma, which like my parents' lock combination has also been colonized, renamed after a white admiral. Now this mountain is known as Mount Rainier. On some of the old maps of Tacoma, you can still see the lines that border this area of the east side, labeled INDIAN ALLOTMENT LAND. This is the reservation. The river is polluted. There are no grocery stores in walking distance, but from the hill we can see downtown. We can look out at the Salish Sea. A white friend once told me he moved his family away from Tacoma because he wanted to have a garden. He wanted to teach his young son how to grow things and he told me, "You can't do that here. The soil is bad."

I made my way to the kitchen. My parents had reno-vated the house with new wood floors, sleek lighting fix-tures, and updated cabinets. The house looked modern, but so many old things still filled the inside. I passed by the laundry room and thought of my ancestor, a woman called Aunt Susie. This part of the house used to be her bedroom. My parents told me that, as an old woman, during her last days Aunt Susie often sat alone and told stories to herself in the traditional language. Whenever I walked by this part of the house, I felt the hairs on my arm stand up. Some houses are haunted by ghosts. Our house hangs on to words and stories.

I found my parents in the dining room. My mom sat with a spread of language books laid out before her, a mosaic of traditional words and old photographs. She was planning the language conference. My dad looked up from his own book and the two of them smiled at me. We made small talk, a recent poetry reading, the book I was working on, my siblings. My mom set a cup of coffee down in front of me and took her place next to my dad across the table. The room was quiet. "I want to know if it is okay that I wear the red paint." I was cautious and slow in my asking. I knew that it was ceremony I was asking for, something sacred.

My mom rose up from the table silently. Without a word she disappeared downstairs as my dad sat quietly across from me.

Naming Ceremony

As I waited, my eyes wandered to the large cedarwood
cabinet against the wall. I've known it since childhood.
It used to stand in my great-grandmother's house, and it
contained cedar baskets, carvings, and small talismans. I
focused on the small doll on the second shelf, the Sasha
Doll. The doll had been gifted to my mother as a child.
My grandmother had to special order it from a Swiss doll
maker based in Germany. There were no Native American dolls when my mother was young. Just Barbie dolls
and baby dolls, blue-eyed and yellow-haired, but my
grandmother had wanted her daughter to have a doll
that resembled her. It was the only doll at the time with
olive-tone skin, dark hair, and brown eyes. The perfect

Indian baby, one my mother could hold truly as her own. Imprinted on the doll's back in bold letters was SASHA. This is how my mother named me. This doll was my first namesake.

When I was a child I was obsessed with the Sasha Doll; I asked to take her to show-and-tell. I was proud of this strange girl, this relic whose name I bore. But I have always been a clumsy girl, and when I brought the doll to my first-grade show-and-tell, I dropped her on the pavement. When I picked her up I saw her arm had broken off. I was beside myself with shock. I picked the pieces up and tried to shove the arm back into its delicate socket. I held the two pieces together with all my might, thinking they might magically fuse back together. *I can fix you*, I thought. *I can fix you.*

To my horror the doll had to be taken to the doll hospital, to mend what had been broken. The doll doctor did what I could not and put her back together again. After she was fixed the doll and I became estranged. I'd failed her. With shame I watched my mother take the doll back and put her on the shelf. I never touched her again.

In addition to the Sasha Doll, the shelf housed cedar baskets, paintings, and old photographs. One photograph in particular my mother had shown me before. It featured a woman in silver and sepia tone standing next to a river. She looked strong. She was proud and sturdy and beautiful. "This is your great-great-grandmother Louise," my mother told me when I was ten. "Your great-great-grandmother." Louise was my middle name. In contrast to the woman in the photograph, I was a pale, distractible thing. Surely there had been a mistake. "You come from a long line of strength," my mother assured me. "You carry it in your name."

The very vessel that held all of these artifacts came from another woman whose name I carry. Louise's daughter, my great-grandmother, Violet taqʷšəblu Hilbert gifted me her Skagit name. To be a namesake is a great responsibility. "You're my namesake and you're going to do important things," she would say to me.

There is a photograph of me at my naming ceremony, small in a blue dress, mess of brown ringlets falling around my face as I teeter precariously close to the edge of a picnic table. The photo was taken in 1986. I am three years old. My arm is outstretched as if reaching for someone out of frame and I'm smiling. I'd like to think it was my great-grandmother just out of reach, coming to gather her namesake up in her arms, but there is no way of knowing. It could have been my mother. It could have been anybody. I have white socks with ruffles and strappy shoes. You can tell from the photo that my mother wanted me to look nice. You can also tell by the grin on my face that moments after the photo was taken I would be barefoot, that my dress would be streaked in grass stains. When remembering that day, my mother sighs, laughs a little, and says, "I looked across the yard, saw you on the table dancing next to a boombox, and I just knew you were going to be a handful."

That day relatives passed me along in their arms. As uncles tended to the fire, as the salmon baked, friends and family tousled my hair, pinched my cheeks, and said things like "taqʷšəblu number two" and "What hard shoes to fill!"

I like to think my great-grandmother knew what she was doing that day, that she knew the countercurse I would someday need. Like the fairy godmother in *Sleeping Beauty* who saved her gift for last and passed to the sleeping princess the only thing that could wake her.

As a child I would long for what princesses possessed: magic, courage, enchanted slippers, and the love of brave princes. I would come to yearn for new worlds and ways to escape. What I wouldn't realize was the power that was bestowed upon me that day, the magic my great-grandmother passed down. And it wasn't true love's kiss. It wasn't a prince. It wasn't a spell or a slipper. It was a name: taqʷšəblu. Like an incantation.

Tock-sha-blue. It comes from deep in me. Travels through parted lips out into the world and stays there.

Linoleum

Three years before I asked my parents about red paint I was riding north with my boyfriend. It was my thirtieth birthday and Brandon and I were driving up the interstate. I watched him drive. Brandon was classically handsome, tall, with cropped dark hair and brown eyes. I'd met him nine years ago at a party. He walked in and I remember thinking, *Damn, a real-life Agent Cooper.* Agent Dale Cooper was the hero of my favorite TV show, *Twin Peaks*, a campy yet surreal series from my childhood that had a cult following. Created by David Lynch, the show was heavy with dark and supernatural themes, often terrifying, and along with Nirvana, responsible for putting this rainy corner of the Pacific Northwest on the map.

I loved the show immediately. It was special to see Washington represented on-screen, to recognize the dense forests and dark bodies of water where I grew up flickering back at me as I watched the show late into the night. The fictionalized town of Twin Peaks was meant to be somewhere near the Canadian border in the northernmost corner of Washington, basically positioning the town in my backyard or, at the very least, neighboring my small reservation. This was not the usual backdrop for a popular television series, and seeing the thick knit sweaters, rainy skies, tall pine trees, logging trucks, and shitty diners made me feel at home. The show made me feel less invisible. There was even a predictable and stereotypical Native American character, Deputy Hawk. Hawk was the source of all the Indian mysticism in the show. He was, of course, a tracker. A turquoise earring dangled from one ear, he wore his dark hair long, and he knew the woods. Besides watching *Dances with Wolves*, this was the first time I had actually seen a real-life Indian character on the screen.

It was Agent Cooper who had my heart, though. Cooper was an intuitive and mystic FBI agent, with transcendental dreams and an affinity for black coffee. Cooper ends up solving the mystery of a murdered high school girl, Laura Palmer, and frees her from the Black Lodge, an evil place that held her spirit captive. I have always wanted an Agent Cooper, and here I'd found him in Brandon.

Tall pine trees and the Cascade Mountains floated by beyond the window. I smiled. It was a good birthday. Brandon's parents were gone for the weekend and we were heading north out of Seattle to take care of their plants and spend a quiet weekend alone. We lived in a collective house with friends, the drummer in Brandon's band and his girlfriend, a photographer I waited tables with. We loved the communal nature of our home, the parties, the bands crashing, the shared spaces always crowded with travelers. The weekend getaway felt special. It felt like playing house. I liked to sit at the fancy dining room table, with matching dish sets and crystal glass. We walked our dog and read by the fireplace. Some part of me got a kick out of the *normalcy*. We drove north and I saw the landscape change. I watched the river snake through the valley alongside the interstate.

——

When my great-grandmother was just a girl she traveled up and down the river with her parents. They traveled by canoe on the Skagit River, her tribe's river. Her father was a fisherman, a logger, an Indian man who knew how to make his living off the river. In the summer they would pick berries, and my great-grandmother would have to attend the Tulalip Indian Boarding School during the berry season. When she told us about the constant moving around, my great-grandmother would smile, even when talking about sleeping in shacks, and walls with no paint, and dirt floors. "My mother traveled with a rolled-up piece of linoleum," she'd recall warmly. "No matter where we were, she'd lay it down, she'd create home wherever she could."

My parents were also nomadic. We moved prompted by similar necessities—money, jobs, a place to fit five kids. It just looked different. We lived in apartments and basements. I grew up used to impermanence. I grew up used to saying goodbye to places. When we moved into the trailer on the Swinomish Reservation it was a temporary home, something impermanent made out of aluminum and particleboard, something without bones.

Our first real plans for a home took shape on a plot of land in the dense woods of the reservation. We put our single-wide trailer on a relative's property while our lot across the street was being cleared. We were told to call him "Uncle," though it was never clear if he was a blood relative or simply related to us in that Indian way. The land wasn't glamorous. There was a garbage pile that sank into the forest on the side of this uncle's double-wide, and a large red metal building where he smoked fish, a meadow behind the smokehouse, and our small, tinny, single-wide trailer, scooted up against the tree line.

"Just find ways to entertain yourselves," my parents would say to my siblings and me before disappearing to their long shifts. My dad worked late hours at the casino, and my mom commuted all the way to Seattle to keep her job there at the group home for native youth. We became accustomed to late nights of movie rentals and frozen pizza, of games of double dare where me or one of my siblings would tear through the trails into the darkness of the woods with no flashlight just to see how far we could make it before we cried out.

The woods of the fictional town of Twin Peaks were also ominous. Like my backyard, they were thick with tall trees, owls, and mysteries. Most of the townspeople of Twin Peaks feared the woods, but not my second-favorite character. Audrey Horne didn't appear to be afraid of anything. And I loved her immediately. She's introduced as Agent Cooper's love interest and the daughter of a corrupt hotel owner, Benjamin Horne. Seventeen-year-old Audrey Horne is dark, smart, and strange. She wears her black hair in a cropped bob, switches from her saddleback shoes to a pair of red pumps hidden in her locker, and smokes in the girls' room. Her father, a possible suspect in her classmate's murder, is a sleazy man, usually shrouded in cigar smoke and a bad suit. As part owner of One Eyed Jacks, a casino and brothel on the other side of the Canadian border, Benjamin Horne has his hands in illegal gambling, underage prostitution, and drugs. Audrey falls for Cooper immediately. And it's not just because he's handsome. She sees the innate goodness within him.

More importantly, she sees him as her ticket out. Audrey decides she wants to help Cooper solve the mystery, which leads her down a dangerous path of running away, going undercover, and eventually getting kidnapped at the very brothel her father owns. Keeping her identity hidden with a masquerade mask, Audrey is nearly assaulted by her father, a scene that made my stomach hurt and my chest tighten. Afterward she runs to a phone. It's the only time you see Audrey in fear. She dials the number and with a shaky voice leaves a message: "Special Agent, why aren't you here?"

I didn't grow up with a corrupt hotel owner as my father, but I was in danger. Our uncle was not rich and did not wear suits or smoke cigars, but he liked to party. On sunny days he'd sit on the porch drinking cans of beer with his friends while the kids went nuts in the front yard over the homemade slip-and-slide he made. He bought me my first two-piece bathing suit on such an afternoon when I complained I didn't have one. I was ten. I didn't want to go careening down a series of garbage bags lined with garden hoses and sprinklers in just my underpants; that was embarrassing. He went out for errands, returning with sodas, bags of Cool Ranch Doritos, and a lime-green, two-piece bathing suit. "Look at that," our uncle would laugh, and I'd hear the pop and hiss of a beer can being opened. "She's got a little bubble butt!"

Perhaps if another adult had been around, a sober

one, my parents maybe, someone would have noticed. Someone could have warned me. But without someone there I was left unattended, unprotected. After a night of babysitting, I fell asleep on our uncle's water bed with his three-year-old daughter. This wasn't unusual. The trailers were just a few short steps from each other. As kids we learned to treat the space between like a hallway. As the credits to Disney's *The Little Mermaid* flickered against the yellowing walls of his bedroom, he stumbled in from the bar. The smell of beer on a lover's breath still bothers me. Not wine, or whiskey, or other spirits. It's the smell of beer that awakens some fear in me. The way it seeps out of the skin, permeates the breath. Sometimes I have had to ask a partner after a night out if they wouldn't mind brushing their teeth. I'm afraid of them seeing me break when they kiss me.

—

After the night on the water bed, I learned to run away. I wanted to find my own Agent Cooper. I cut my dark hair short and started wearing fire-engine-red lipstick. I slept in bowling alleys and on friends' couches. Once, I even slept in an empty Petco under construction. A few friends and I hopped the fence, climbed a massive pile of wooden pallets, and slept until the gray light of morning crept in through the unfinished walls and woke us.

That morning I met a boy in the parking lot, old enough to buy cigarettes and old enough to rent a hotel room. He was working on one of the buildings, probably the Petco, and said I could stay with him. I wanted a warm place to sleep. I wanted a bed and company. That night I went with him back to his hotel room. Pink walls and an orange carpet dotted with old cigarette burns made up the landscape of the small room. The boy had a shaved head, with a purple lock of hair that fell down over one side of his face, and a nose ring. He popped beer cans open and chain-smoked, told me about bands and about living in Portland. Then he asked if he could see me undressed. I drank two beers back-to-back to work up the courage, then nervously slipped out of my clothes. My exposed body felt bare and vulnerable. This was my only currency. I stood there, fifteen and shivering against a pale pink wall tinged yellow from years of cigarette smoke. I trembled a little and crawled into the hotel bed. The boy just looked at my body, ran his hands over it, and eventually passed out. In the morning I left. I knew I needed to find something else. The hotel was not a home and the boy was no special agent.

—

I have always wanted a permanent home, a place to feel safe. The rooms I'd occupy as I grew into adulthood were always adorned with the relics I carried with me. A can of salmon gifted to me by my grandmother, stones, candles, a photograph of my mother and me, these things were my linoleum.

Years after my teenage homelessness, I learned how to take care of myself. I learned to work, to pay bills, to pay rent. I even went to college. Still, I searched for home, I searched for my special agent. I wanted some place I could truly call mine.

I fell in love with Brandon from across a room at a party after a punk show. He was the most handsome man I had ever seen up close. He wasn't mean when he drank, he picked me up whenever I called, drew me baths, made me hot chocolate. I felt I'd found my Agent Cooper.

But like Audrey, I was doomed. I was a little bit broken, and I tried to hide that from him. I kept my secrets. I put on the red lips and an assumed fearlessness. I wanted to be the kind of girl Agent Cooper could fall for. And like Audrey's, my plan worked for a while. Brandon fell under my spell and I believed I had found my home.

———

On my thirtieth birthday we drove up the highway and I looked out at the mountains and the fog in the trees. I knew that if we kept going we would eventually hit the small town next to the reservation, then beyond that the trailer, and finally those dark woods. When we got to his parents' house that evening, Brandon made my favorite dinner, something I had grown up eating: smoked salmon and pasta with Alfredo sauce. As a kid I thought this food was fancy. I didn't realize we ate it because pasta was cheap and we had smoked salmon in surplus. Still, this meal remained my favorite. After dinner we sipped champagne. He brought out dessert, a chocolate-ice-cream cookie sandwich, and sitting on top was a diamond ring.

I said yes. He had been my family, my home, he had been my something permanent. When I looked down at the ring, I was far away from basements, hotels, bowling alleys, and empty Petco buildings. I was far away from trailers and water beds. When I looked at that ring I saw a home wherever I was. I saw my great-grandmother's linoleum.

Spirit Sickness

We spent the summer engaged, wondering how a wedding would work. At the time, I was attending the Institute of American Indian Arts in Santa Fe. We decided that I would fly back there, complete my undergraduate degree, and return the following summer. We'd get married on the solstice. That would give us the school year to plan.

As my flight made its final descent I spun the ring on my finger in slow circles and I thought of the word "wife."

"Is that an engagement ring?" My friend Kali sat next to me in our Intro to Jewelry and Metals class. I was comically bad at making jewelry, but it was a good repose from the work I was doing in our nonfiction and poetry classes. It felt good to saw through things, hammer things, bend things, and watch things glow and change in the fire. Plus our instructor was cool, looked like Nick Cave, and let us listen to Bikini Kill.

Kali rushed over to my side of our shared worktable and gently picked my hand up in hers. "It's beautiful," she said smiling up at me, "congratulations." I just blushed, embarrassed. I never felt like the kind of person who would ever get married. I happily existed in a nontraditional relationship. For the past year I'd also been dating a woman, openly and with Brandon's blessing. This arrangement allowed me to feel independent, free-spirited, queer, punk, all things that challenged my conception of the title of "wife." I also lived in an entirely different state most of the year; I existed on my own terms, my own schedule and rules. I wondered if being a wife would somehow change all of that. Would it change everything?

—

The semester following my engagement I began writing about my trauma for the first time. If becoming a wife wasn't going to change me, the work I was about to unlock in my creative nonfiction class certainly would. And I had no idea. The assignment was to write a personal essay exploring our most traumatic memory. It took me a weekend and a bottle of wine to complete the assignment.

Afterward, I closed my eyes and saw dozens of little boats floating along the ceiling, against the yellowing wallpaper of a small trailer in the middle of the woods on the Swinomish Reservation. The day the assignment was due we went around the table sharing. I listened as my classmates recounted memories of their pets and loved ones dying, of driving across the country, starting a new school, leaving their homes and family behind. I held my essay, sweaty in my hands, terrified to read what I had written, to say out loud what had happened to me.

My instructor pulled me aside that day to check in but also to tell me how powerful she thought the writing was. At the time, I was also writing stories about mermaids, selkies, and witches. I wanted to write poetry and magical realism. But that day my instructor encouraged me to put that all aside. She told me to dig deeper into the memory of the little boats. I went back to the house after school and pulled a box of photos from my closet. I wanted to find her, the girl I had been before that night in Swinomish on the water bed, the girl with a mess of brown waves falling into her face, wide-eyed and smiling.

I found photos of me climbing trees, standing by the ocean, and sitting on my great-grandmother's lap next to a roaring fire. Then I found photos of me in latex skirts, with a shaved head, sporting blue lipstick, and wearing a dog collar. I found photos of me at the alternative high school I would eventually drop out of, of me skateboarding and drinking beer, and of the first boyfriend I had that I wasn't afraid of.

—

Richard and I met outside the Vasa Hall in Mount Vernon. Mount Vernon was the closest town to the reservation, and I had become accustomed to hitchhiking there to escape and hang out with friends. But this was different. It was Halloween and I was at my first punk show. I was fourteen, and I hadn't been home in days. Some friends and I had taken a taxi to the all-ages show. The three of us wore torn fishnets, black lipstick, and glittering tiaras. We didn't really step out of the cab so much as tumble out in a pile. Jack Daniel's was coursing through me so intensely my veins felt like liquid fire. I watched my breath puff out like smoke into the cold night, poisoned and euphoric.

The cab sped away, leaving us in the parking lot surrounded by faces caked in white paste, mouths oozing the peppermint smell of fake blood, loud music, and bodies that slammed against one another. There were leather jackets and boots everywhere, cigarette smoke, and smuggled beers.

Swaying a little, I adjusted my tiara and pulled my black slip down over my knees. That's when I spotted him. Richard. His moss-green eyes found me in the dark.

As I stumbled through the crowd I saw his face, pale and freckled beneath a streetlight. He sat, a nymphlike creature along the wall. He wasn't yelling or smashing cans of beer with his boot; he was quiet, strange, and special. He looked directly at me, but his gaze didn't do what other boys' gazes did. It didn't creep into my stomach and nauseate me. Instead it found a deeper me and stayed there. *I want to be close to that*, I thought. *He's like magic.* I stumbled directly to him and fell like confetti around him. Even the way he sat seemed gentle: his thin frame against the wall, black-clad head to toe and knees pulled up to his chest.

"Hello." His voice was soft, but deep, and he smiled a timid smile.

"You look like that one guy." I adjusted my slip and hiccupped. "From that one band . . . sort of. But prettier." I stumbled over my words drunkenly.

"Is that so?" He laughed kindly, patiently.

As ghosts in studded vests and zombies in army jackets pushed and shoved past us, we talked about David Lynch and Sylvia Plath. We talked about hating school and going to concerts, and my hand found his in the dark. His older brother was playing Misfits cover songs inside and I felt Richard might get up at any moment. I had to act fast.

"I like you." I wanted it to sound more like destiny and less like Jack Daniel's. But it sort of fell out of my mouth. So there it was. I moved my body closer to his, but he made no advances. I touched his face with my fingers, and he blushed a little bit. I wanted to kiss him.

"You've had a lot to drink, haven't you?" He shifted his eyes away and sighed. I was confused. *Hell yes, I've had a lot to drink*, I thought. Wasn't that a good thing? I wore my delinquency with pride, like some sort of fucked-up Girl Scout badge. I shrugged and gave my best zero-fucks-given face. His expression softened, but his face and hands remained off my body.

Fuck, I thought, as he sat composed next to me, *I'm too wasted to be talking to this dude. He's too smart.* Right away, from the moment he spoke to me at that punk show on Halloween, Richard made me want to be ... better.

—

With the small photograph still in my hand, I snapped out of the past, hurled into the present by an incoming text. It was Brandon. He wanted to know when I was coming home for midwinter break. I booked a flight and texted him the details, then I began putting the photos away. One fell to the floor and I leaned over to pick it up. Four generations of Coast Salish women stared back at me. My mother, my grandmother, and my great-grandmother stood together, smiling for the camera. I'm small and in the center of the photo, held by my grand-mother, also smiling. I put the rest of the photographs away but kept this one out, propped against a book on my bedside table.

I went to bed with their faces in my mind, and that night I dreamt of walking. I walked north in the woods along the Skagit River. I stepped barefoot through the trees, the dirt and twigs cold against my skin. I came to a clearing and found a porcelain pedestal sink in the center. I stepped up to the ornate faucet that looked like it was from another time. Floating above it was an oval mirror. I shivered against the cold breeze that rustled through the cedar and fir. Then a voice spoke to me, but not in a language I understood. The voice spoke in the traditional language, perhaps one even older than that. Though I couldn't understand, I listened anyway. I stared at the mirror, at the face reflected back, which was old and un-recognizable. A woman from another time looked back at me, holding a wool blanket over her shoulders. Then I dunked my head into the sink full of freezing water and opened my mouth.

I woke up screaming. It was six in the morning and I didn't have to be on campus for hours. Pacing back and forth as the desert sun came through my window in beams of golden light, I concentrated on the face I had seen in the mirror. Too unsettled to sleep, I made coffee. Piles of poems and writing assignments littered my desk, and I began sifting through them. I tried to busy myself with schoolwork, but I couldn't shake the feeling of cold water rushing down the back of my throat. I was used to nightmares—they became a recurring thing in my childhood. But this one felt different. In the nightmares I had when I was younger, I was always being chased, hunted, or hurt. I felt the weight of a man above me, dark and shadowlike. I shuddered when I thought of those nightmares, remembering how they got worse when I was a teenager. This dream felt different, scary in a way I didn't recognize. The woman in the mirror had been so clear, so familiar.

An hour before I was supposed to be in class I remembered where I had seen the face and went to my bookshelf. Next to the Lushootseed dictionary compiled by my great-grandmother was the book I was looking for. I pulled it off the shelf and stared at the cover. The book's title was *The Wisdom of a Skagit Elder*. Lushootseed text was printed above a photograph of a woman's face, and listed beneath was an English name: Susie Sampson Peter. Aunt Susie. My parents had a portrait of her on their wall when I was a child. I had grown up seeing this book, which was a collection of transcriptions of conversations between Susie and my great-grandmother. Aunt Susie was my great-grandmother's aunt and she was a medicine worker, one of the first women in our tribe trained in that way. I had heard stories of her as a small child, faced with impossible tasks. She had crossed the Skagit River, in the middle of the night, at ten years old, in only her undergarments. She had canoed to Smith Island off Whidbey, by herself, where she found her spirit power. Aunt Susie was strong, I remembered that much, and Aunt Susie probably wore red paint.

The noise of my roommates bustling around the house, making coffee and getting ready for the day, reminded me I needed to get to campus, so I shoved the book back on the shelf and rushed to class. On the short drive through the desert I thought of Aunt Susie and my great-grandmother. I pictured them up together in the small room in the back of the house on the reservation in Tacoma, Washington. My great-grandmother with her tape recorder and Aunt Susie with her stories.

—

I wrote and revised the Little Boats essay. I fell into it, and it took hold of me. Over the weeks, it grew and expanded. Slowly it took hold of my life and I fell deeper, giving it more of myself. Each page I wrote awakened new nightmares. I absentmindedly scribbled little boats on the corners of my notebook pages. I was becoming haunted. Spirit-sick.

Back in Seattle for midwinter break, things got worse. The essay became my thesis. The thesis became a book idea. I was frozen in time, in memories. I put them down on paper when they came, thinking that this was enough. But I was reckless with memory and trauma. Flashbacks of not only the first assault but ones that happened years later began to torment me. I had excavated the bones of these memories, unaware that they would reanimate, that they would chase me into dreams. The bones took shape in these flashbacks. The day a boy with a skateboard fed me drinks and took me to the woods came back to me. The memory of him not allowing me to leave until I let him push me up against a rock and pull up my skirt flooded my dreams like a tidal wave. At the time, I didn't know that this was rape; I thought it was just something I had to do to get safely back to the apartment I lived in. And they didn't stop there. When the nightmares followed me into my waking hours I had no idea what to do, and neither did Brandon.

Still, I tried to channel Audrey Horne, dark, smart, and most of all fearless. I behaved as usual. We were a happy, functional couple, glowing in the light of our recent engagement. Our friends seemed delighted to help with our wedding plans. Even my girlfriend was coming to the wedding. We laughed about grotesque wedding dresses dripping in lace and crinoline. Life carried on as usual. But one night I was yanked out of my charade by something I had not expected.

"What did I do?" Brandon's face was close to mine. Rain hammered down against the windows of our Seattle home. I couldn't recall how we got to this moment, but I was screaming and shaking.

The last thing I could remember was us in bed, listening to records and drinking wine, giddy over our engagement. I remembered a kiss, followed by a deeper kiss. Then I blacked out, and not the kind of blackout from drugs or alcohol. It was like I left my body involuntarily. Disoriented, I tried to take inventory of the objects around me, as if to count the things in the physical space in order to return to it. I saw my suitcases, my school bags. I saw my surroundings, my fiancé. I was safe.

"Where did you go, just now?" Brandon asked.

I wrapped my arms around him and pulled him close. "I'm here, I'm sorry. I'm here."

But I wasn't, not fully. I had sunk down into a memory; the weight of a man's body above me had caused me to retreat inward. I was lost in the memory of being assaulted. Brandon was kissing me, then his hand slid up my arm, to my wrist. It was gentle, but it tripped some wire in me. All of a sudden, I was a teenager again. I blinked, and the teenage boy who had pushed me up against a boulder in the woods after he had several beers was above me. I felt the twigs and the rough rock against my cheek.

This had happened before, fifteen years earlier with Richard. As teenagers we hid out in a friend's spare room, spending almost every night together. Experimenting with safety and intimacy with Richard unlocked the memory of the little boats, and I woke screaming and beating my fists against him in the middle of the night. When I came to, he was staring at me, holding me, his eyes flashing with fear and sympathy as he tried to console me, as he tried to push back against a monster he couldn't even see. I loved him for it, for trying to keep the boats at bay, but I was sick—my spirit was not there.

My tribe believes in a kind of spirit sickness. When your spirit is angry, or distressed, it can leave you. It abandons you, and when it does you can sometimes lose consciousness. Over time you become sick. You lose interest in things, start to sleep a lot, you grow cold and no number of blankets will warm you. Eventually you lie down and never wake.

—

I had been sick several years ago, when we lost my great-grandmother. As her namesake I felt part of myself try to leave with her, to the spirit world. Brandon had also been with me then.

The last time I saw my great-grandmother was in the middle of a terrible snowstorm. My mother had called me at work. "You need to be here. Now." I quickly untied my apron and ran out of the restaurant. Brandon and I had been dating for a year. He offered to drive me. My grandmother's house was an hour north of the city. I was panicked the entire way. The farther we got from Seattle, the more treacherous the storm became. Just outside of the Swinomish Reservation, a semitruck was jackknifed on the highway ahead of us. Brandon knew how to handle his truck in the snow, but his skill did little to calm my anxiety. The snow piled on the windshield. There was a silence in the cab of the truck that can only occur in winter when snow mutes the world. The only sound was the swoosh of the windshield wipers bringing the highway back into view again and again. I sucked in a shallow breath and my lungs felt rushed. He asked if I had my inhaler. I did. I closed my eyes and pressed my head against the window. I tried to imagine that the world on the other side was safe.

The afternoon I first introduced Brandon to my great-grandmother he was shy and I had to scoot him forward to shake her hand. Her eyes were already bad then, and he had to get close. She looked up at me and asked, "What color is he, dear?"

"Grandma," I smiled, embarrassed, "you can't say that!" She just chuckled and held his hand in hers.

"Is he a nice Indian boy?"

"Grandma!" I tried to hush her, but the room was already laughing. "No, Grandma, Brandon is not native." I looked sheepishly to my new, now terrified, boyfriend.

"Well, as long as he doesn't bore you." She released his hand and smiled warmly in his direction. "Don't you bore my great-granddaughter. She's my namesake." The room was full of family members and laughter. Even Brandon looked suddenly at ease. But some part of me retreated. Some part of me questioned if I was somehow losing something. *Was I disappointing her? Because I'm part white? Because I'm dating a white man? Am I becoming less Indian? Would I lose my Indianness completely?* I thought of our someday children. I thought of them unable to enroll in our tribe. I thought of them never meeting their great-great-grandmother or hearing our tribe's stories in our traditional language.

In the truck my breath fogged patterns on the glass. A transformer somewhere above exploded, raining electric-blue sparks down onto the white world. Cars alongside the freeway sunk into the snow. I rocked back and forth and sucked in air. I kept my eyes closed until I couldn't take it anymore. My hand shot toward the handle. "Stop the truck!" My chest sputtered with asthma and my heart drummed. "This isn't safe. Look at those cars. Nobody is driving out here. Nobody is on the road." In the cab of the truck I was a wide-eyed and feral thing. Brandon put the child lock on and calmly touched my shoulder, but I was angry. Mad at him like he was somehow causing the snow. Mad at him for offering to brave the roads. Mad at him like he somehow had control over anything.

"We have to keep going," he said. "We're so close." I knew he was right, and he knew it wasn't the snow I was afraid of. He knew that in twenty minutes we would arrive. I rode the rest of the way with my head in my hands. I didn't want to see the mile markers, the familiar farms, the channel, the recognizable world of my childhood blanketed in white.

With my eyes closed I thought of her voice, the low, guttural sounds of our traditional language. I remembered the stories she told while I was growing up. I remembered the last meal we shared: oysters.

Brandon safely pulled the truck in front of my great-grandmother's home. "We're here."

I sat with my hand on the door watching the snowfall in the streetlight. Brandon walked around the truck and opened the door, and I fell out into the cold night, against him. We walked up the icy steps and my mom opened the door. Inside, everything glowed warm and orange. Cedar baskets lined the walls of my great-grandmother's small apartment and candles burned pink lights around us. Here we were, four generations of women: my mother, my grandmother, me, and my great-grandmother, who looked small and frail. I lingered in the doorway with a lump in my throat, unable to move my legs until Brandon guided me slowly toward the pullout sofa where my great-grandmother lay dying.

She had been teaching Lushootseed again. Books and papers were scattered around the apartment. Lushootseed words scribbled in marker, big and black, filled yellow legal pads. My great-grandmother wore a purple terry-cloth robe and I noticed how it matched the Gatorade that my mom delicately lifted to her face. She sipped slowly, then lay back down. My mom motioned for me to come closer and I did, lying down beside my great-grandmother on the mattress. Quiet filled the room, not the cold silence beyond the window of winter or snow-covered mountains but the silence of how I imagine the buds of flowers must be before they open. Looking at the pink glow from the candlelight, the orange cedar of the baskets, and the purple liquid gleaming in the small glass at my great-grandmother's lips, I thought of spring. Her fingers wrapped around mine delicately, the skin translucent like petals. Outside the world was white and frozen, but inside I looked at the faces of the women in the room, four generations all huddled quietly in the warmth. It felt like a hearth. It felt like abundance.

"You should really get going, dear," my mom looked out the window, then to Brandon. "It's not going to stop."

I glared out the window at the snow already piling on the hood of the truck. Brandon looked concerned. He mentioned to my mom and grandmother that I panicked in the truck, that I tried to open the door on the freeway. I didn't want to let go of my great-grandmother's hand and started to feel my breath go shallow again. With help, I stood. My grandmother hugged me, then my mother. They gave me a small, white pill for the ride home.

"It's for anxiety," my grandmother told me. I looked down at the thing in my hand, then back to my great-grandmother, and nodded.

Outside Brandon helped me to the truck. He fastened my seat belt. I pulled his hand close and held it. All I could mutter was a simple "Thank you."

The roads twisted and curved through the snow-covered farm flats. In springtime these fields were lined with rows of primary-colored tulips, attracting carloads of tourists. I wondered what indigenous flowers grew in this valley before the land was colonized. I tried to imagine what the land must have looked like when my great-grandmother was a girl, before dikes and farmhouses.

"I'll never hear her tell me a story in Lushootseed again," I said while staring out the window. I looked at the white pill in the palm of my hand, bit it in half, and tasted the bitter, metallic flavor on my tongue.

I got the call somewhere outside of Everett. "She's gone." My mom's voice dissolved through the phone and the drug in my bloodstream. I didn't cry. Instead, I swallowed the other half of the pill. I leaned my head against the window and stared at the winter beyond, whiting out the world. I closed my eyes and hoped for sleep. I tried not to think of the long wait ahead, of waiting out winter. I tried to tell myself that spring was just around the corner.

My spirit left me then, and for many days all I did was sleep. I called into work. I kicked the covers away from my body. I tossed and turned. The curtains weren't dark enough, so I learned to ignore the daylight. Some mornings I heard Brandon at the stove, heating water for tea, trying to get me to eat. I could almost get to him. I could almost get back to the world. But a wave would crash over me and my room would fill with water again and again, reminding me I was still asleep. Never waking, I got lonely. I chased a speck of paint, like a white rabbit, across the bedroom wall, convinced if I followed it long enough it would lead me back to the waking world. But my eyes were too heavy, and I lost the speck of paint again and fell deeper into slumber. I slept days and weeks away. I slept my body sore. I slept through several bill cycles, and eventually my mother called.

"You can't sleep like that," she told me. "You need to see a healer. A medicine worker. You need to wake up."

In the months that followed, my mother took me to our medicine worker, the same one who had been with us at Great-grandmother's burning ceremony. Burning ceremonies are done to help prepare those we have lost for their journey to the spirit world. We burn their clothes, their belongings, their favorite food. Anything that might help them on their way. Great-grandma was hanging out, reluctant to pass on, reluctant perhaps to leave us, so we had gathered in the field behind her house at the fire pit. My uncle and father stoked a bonfire, while people inside the house prepared food. As we stood around the fire waiting for the ceremony, my dad put an arm around me. "Crazy," he said. "Isn't it strange that just fifty years ago we'd be arrested for this? Charged with witchcraft."

When the ceremony started I was stable, sturdy, and standing upright. I was strong and able to face it, but by the time the songs started I began to feel weak. I began to tremble. I saw plates of food stacked onto the fire and burning away. I saw salmon, potato salad, and fry bread as it blackened and disappeared. I saw my mother bent over the fire, carefully pouring a tiny glass of purple Gatorade into the flames. She did this as gently as she had when she brought it to my great-grandmother's lips the night she died. Something in me gave out. Like a string that had been pulling me upright had snapped. Like a marionette cut down, I fell. The world went cold. It was winter, it was cold. But all of a sudden, the cold got inside me, found its way into my bones. I shivered as I fell apart next to the fire. I desperately wanted to yank the sweaters, the plates of food, her belongings, things she had touched one by one from the fire and cling to them, to hold them to my chest, to clutch their warmth until they turned to ash in my hands. I frantically looked around the field for my great-grandmother. I was sure she would come for me, to collect me, to take me away with her, because surely I had died out here. But no spirit came for me.

The medicine worker had witnessed this. He had felt her spirit clinging to me the way they sometimes do. "If they stay too long," he explained to me, "you can get very sick." The work he did on me was to help her move on, to help me move on.

After seeing the healer, my mom and I drove home from the tribal center. She reminded me that I come from a long line of strength. "Grandma?" I asked, still feeling her absence in my chest when I said it aloud. "And Aunt Susie?" My mom nodded, but she also reminded me about the woman called Comptia. Years earlier my mom had told me the story of a woman who lived on the southern coast of Washington. Comptia fled her village following a smallpox epidemic that had claimed the lives of her loved ones. Alone for the first time, she married a settler, a Scottish sea captain of the Hudson Bay Trading Company. The captain had learned that any white settler marrying an Indian woman received twice the allotment of land, though she was not permitted to live in the same house. He made her a small shack with a dirt floor, four walls, and one window.

"How strong would you have to be to survive something like that?" My mom asked it aloud, but I didn't answer. That's when she reminded me that Comptia's blood was my blood. "You're a direct descendant."

But that night as I trembled in bed, as the record still spun, as the rain hammered down, as my fiancé brushed the sweat and hair from my face, I felt far away from my body. Whatever strength supposedly coursed through my veins was dormant. If I had something inside of me at all, it was hidden, out of reach.

Ships, 1828

She walked the trail along the coastline, where the river became the sea. A familiar path rose and fell as it curved along the large stones of the seashore. Her bare feet padded along the wet earth.

Comptia lived in a small fishing village on the coast. She was of the Chinook people. Her village was made up of large plank houses; the largest, the longhouse, was for spirit work, dances. Canoes came ashore along the river, where women, elders, and children worked when the men were away. They wove cedar baskets, they wove mats for sleeping and garments. They harvested berries and shellfish.

Comptia knew the path. She had memorized the places where it opened up to the rocky beach or forked inward and climbed back into the forest. With the woven strap of her cedar basket hanging off her arm, she walked to the fresh spring where she would fill her basket with water.

Through a break in the trees Comptia saw the open ocean. Floating there were several large mountains. The mountains seemed to have grown up overnight. She saw their massive bodies breaking through the surface of the water and climbing into the sky. Their strange snowcaps thin and waving in the breeze.

From her vantage she watched the things move and sway, realizing they weren't mountains at all but huge canoes. She saw men moving, saw them lowering smaller canoes down into the water. She watched as they boarded them, lowering bags one by one down into the small boats.

Comptia, at eight years old, already knew a lot of things. She knew where to gather clams for eating, how to harvest camas, and where to pick the best berries. But she did not know who those men on board the ships were. She did not know all the things they would bring ashore with them. Things she had never seen or heard of: gold, whiskey, smallpox.

As she made her way back to the village, she had no way of knowing that the disease the men in the ships brought with them would eventually wipe out her family and nearly the entire population of the Chinook people in 1829.

Blanket-Wrapping Ceremony

"Your dad and I ordered you your wedding blanket," my mom's voice came through my earbuds as I sat at my desk in the creative writing studio at school. I was going to be married in the traditional way. My mother would sing her spirit song. Then my husband and I would be wrapped in a large Pendleton blanket as my father said a blessing. This is how Coast Salish marriages happen.

After midwinter break everything felt more real, the timeline had been set, invitations sent. Planning everything over the phone had its challenges, and tension between Brandon and me manifested itself in short, often frustrating phone conversations between my classes and his work and band practices. We argued about little things—table arrangements, groomsmen attire—and we couldn't decide where to go for a honeymoon. I had saved a big chunk of a scholarship to put toward the wedding, but stretching it far enough for a trip would be difficult. Still, it was important to me that we go somewhere together. I hadn't really traveled since starting school four years earlier. I was desperate for an adventure, and Brandon and I needed the opportunity to reconnect as our relationship entered a new phase. I wanted to go to Ireland. Falling in love with a guy in a punk band brought me to places I never thought I'd be able to go. I had been to Europe before on tours, and I had seen fourteen or more different countries. I had loved Spain and France and had seen beautiful beaches. But now I wanted to see castle ruins, rolling green hills, and rain-swept cliffsides. I wanted to go to the Forty Foot outside of Dublin and jump into the ocean. I pictured us in quaint rooms by the coast, sipping whiskey and kissing next to a fire. Brandon wanted to go to Belize. He compromised on Ireland for the honeymoon, and I promised to make traveling someplace tropical our next priority as a married couple.

As frustrating as it was, planning a wedding and honeymoon was a good reprieve from the work I'd come home to do, late in the night. I had my heart set on attending the graduate program at IAIA, and "Little Boats" was going to be my MFA thesis. I was determined to wrestle my demons into art. But with each page came new memories, new nightmares. I was slowly unlocking a Pandora's box, without any tools or instructions on how to close it again.

My memory felt like a parlor trick most times. I remembered some things, but when a memory was too difficult it vanished like magic. Trauma is funny like that. One night I was up late reworking a chapter, when my thoughts kept returning to Richard. There was something so strange and special about that first love. It was innocent and fragile. He had been so careful with me. With the nightmares returning, it was like reliving my teen years all over again, and a massive gratitude had begun to swell up in me and I wanted Richard to know. At fifteen I was a really messed-up kid who self-medicated to deal with PTSD. I ran away from feelings that brought me into my body and made me stay there. I ran away from Richard and broke his heart. I sent him the first essay, the one that sparked Little Boats. It was half confession, half apology letter. I wanted him to know how much he meant to me. I was surprised when he responded kindly, because after I dumped him I immediately started dating his older brother, a bully with a mohawk and a skateboard who used to torment Richard. He called him names like "faggot" and "pussy." He made fun of the music we loved and the way we dressed. We made an unlikely couple, but his insults only made me crave his approval more. I accepted mixtapes from him, wore his band T-shirts, and followed him like a battered puppy. I didn't feel like Richard owed me kindness, but he gave it to me anyway.

After I sent him the first essay, Richard and I started emailing each other. We caught up on our lives, the art he was making, the writing I was doing. A slow and cautious bridge began to form between us. He was my historian. When my memory failed, he was there to remind me of the details. When he saw the news of my engagement, he wrote to me, "So, are you going to be Mrs. Jones now?" Then he congratulated me, said he never stopped caring for me, after all these years, and said he felt a sort of peace in my engagement. "I always liked Brandon," he admitted. "I was happy to see you with someone who deserved to be with you, who I trusted with you." His blessing meant more than I thought it would, and Richard and I grew closer.

Still, the haunting memories that came with Little Boats persisted. I felt myself adrift in an ocean of nightmares and flashbacks, and I tried to tether myself to the stories of my great-grandmother, Aunt Susie, and now this woman named Comptia. Each chance I got, I asked my mom to tell me more about the woman from the coast. She sent me letters, family histories, and newspaper articles. The more I learned about her, the more grounded and strong I felt.

Spring break arrived and I made a quick trip home to spend a few days with Brandon. A friend from Berlin was visiting, and we met for drinks before seeing some bands play on Capitol Hill. We chatted about wedding plans, graduation, and my MFA program, and eventually the topic of Ireland came up.

"That should be fun," my friend said between sips of his pint, "and, Brandon, your band is going to Australia too?"

I almost spit out my cocktail. I wiped my mouth with the back of my sleeve and looked at my fiancé, looking back at me. If he felt guilty, it was only for a fleeting moment. His face went from surprised to defensive before he could even swallow his beer. "You knew that," he said with an arrogant smirk, shaking his head. But I didn't. We both knew I didn't. Before the engagement, he mentioned that his band was planning a tour to Australia, but I had asked him to reconsider. His tours had taken precedence over us traveling together before. Three summers ago, he had bailed on a trip to Spain, Germany, and England at the last minute. He told me over a bowl of pho at our favorite Vietnamese restaurant on a rainy afternoon. All he said was "I can't go, the band wants to tour Europe, and I can't afford to do both." Just like that. I tried to push the feelings of rejection down into my gut. After all, I fell in love with a musician, and more than that, I fell in love with a guy who played in punk bands. I was used to this sort of thing. I tried to ignore the nagging voice in my head that told me he chose something other than me, that

I didn't deserve his attention, his time, or his love. I took the monthlong trip alone. But here, at the bar in front of our friends, I was ruined. I was being taken for granted, left behind, tricked, trapped. I couldn't ignore it. I looked at him, for the first time, as an enemy. Comptia's story ran through my mind. Had she looked at the Scottish sea captain like this, too? Still, she married him. Why? I couldn't escape the question.

We fought about Australia for the rest of my visit. I wasn't allowed to go on the Australia tour. His current bandmates had a strict no-girlfriends rule, and I guess that applied to partners of nearly a decade and fiancées as well. I thought the rule was stupid. I had joined Brandon on tour before. I knew how to pull my weight, sell merch, help out. I prided myself as a pretty decent roadie. He felt unsupported by me, his fiancée who had fallen into her own ghost story. He wanted me to be stronger, to be *okay*. I felt tricked by him. We couldn't win. I wanted to support his art, but I also wanted to feel chosen. I wanted us to have our own adventure. We settled on another compromise: He would ask his bandmates about me jumping on for the Australia tour. In exchange, I would give up on my dream of a romantic rainy getaway to Ireland. It was more important that we be together.

Back on campus I was becoming a shell, smoothed out, pale, and empty. The memories, the nightmares, and the flashbacks robbed me of rest. I was scared of what I had woken inside of me. I saw my assaults when I closed my eyes. I saw the boys from my childhood, the men, the monsters, every night when I tried to sleep. I had convinced myself that the wedding would wake me from my night terrors, but as I raced to finish my thesis, I found myself growing closer with Richard. Some nights we messaged each other until the sun came up. It felt like time travel, like if I could somehow go back to us, I could fix what had broken. I could at least fix something.

It was a beautiful ceremony. We were married at Brandon's family's cabin in the Cascades. The sun was not yet behind the mountains and the valley was ablaze with golden light. The laughter of wedding guests and the cheerful sounds of our friends and family echoed through the mountains. It was the solstice and everyone felt the length of the day, the warmth, the light that went from golden to amber. A small girl played with my dog across the meadow. Music floated up through the trees. Wildflowers were in bloom and cottonwood seeds floated down like snowflakes. The whole scene was a fairy tale come to life. The tribe donated salmon, and our friends and family feasted together. I threw my bouquet as "Rebel Girl" by Bikini Kill played, and Brandon peeled the light blue lace garter belt off my thigh in the meadow. It was tossed into our crowd of eligible bachelor friends over Leonard

Cohen's "I'm Your Man." But as we were wrapped in our blanket, as my mother hit her drum and sang her traditional song, I felt a crippling anxiety. Something still haunted me. It was like the pitch black of a hallway in the middle of the night when you can't find the light switch. Something was missing. I thought again of Comptia and the captain, and I let myself wonder, *Am I marrying the right person?* Was Brandon my permanence, my home?

Toward the end of the evening, I sat barefoot with Richard in the meadow. The lace of my wedding dress fanned out along the grass. I'd invited him because of our rekindled bond, and as I looked at my friend, my childhood love, looking at the mountains, a nagging uncertainty tugged at me. "Do you think I'm doing the right thing?" I asked him.

"I really like Brandon" was his answer.

I sighed. I felt a love in my heart too big to forget, a safety, a gratitude. I had been so hungry for his approval. When I said goodbye to him, I told him I had always loved him and that I always would. He told me he knew that.

—

After the reception, I drowned. People say when you die, you have an out-of-body experience. Sometimes there's a tunnel, that typical glow waiting for you in the distance. Sometimes you float above yourself, knocking along the ceiling. Sometimes you shake hands with your grandmother. But when I drowned in the Jacuzzi on my wedding night, I didn't have an out-of-body experience. Maybe I hadn't actually died. Maybe I didn't stay dead long enough for tunnels of light and floating and ancestors. But if I had, I imagine I would have seen myself, suspended in water. I might have almost looked beautiful. A water nymph. My waves of hair fanned out like black sea kelp around my made-up face. The hourglass of my form weightless. The lace wedding dress piled up along the side of the tub like a mountain of snowflakes. My new husband, sleeping soundly, legs tucked beneath him on the pillowed bench below the window, an arm's length away from the body of his drowned bride.

But I didn't see any of that. I didn't leave my body. Instead, Brandon woke to the gurgling choke of swallowed water. He leapt from the bench and yanked me like a waterlogged rag doll from the tub. Water sputtered from my lips, stars burst around the corners of my eyes. Brandon shook me. "What the fuck, Sasha, what the fuck!?"

"I'm sorry" was all I could whisper. "I didn't mean to." He wrapped clean hotel towels around me and tucked me into bed.

It was true. I hadn't meant to drown. After the wedding, we danced and crawled all over the honeymoon suite like proper newlyweds. We drank champagne and the river rushed outside our window beneath the stars. At the end of the night we were both exhausted and drunk. I drew a bath and sank into the heat of it. Brandon sat on a bench next to the tub and listened as I sipped wine and started talking.

I talked about my childhood growing up on the reservation. I talked about sexual abuse, assault, and date rape. I talked about the time a line cook put his hands down my pants when I was fourteen. I talked until we were both slipping into sleep and the bathwater swallowed me. The next morning Brandon scolded me again about the dangers of falling asleep in the bath. Then he said, "I had no idea all of that had happened to you. You never told me that."

In the north Cascades we sat as newlyweds in the nook of our bed-and-breakfast. We shared pastries and champagne next to a big window that looked down onto the Wenatchee River. I watched it rush and tumble before us. Sunlight spilled in warm and golden through the trees. Birds sang, and the rich smell of cedar floated on a breeze. I wanted to be light and bubbly like the champagne I was sipping. I wanted to feel the joy I was certain was in me. But I couldn't look away from the white waters of the river as they fought their way through felled trees and branches, as they broke over boulders and carved the forest floor into something deep and ancient. All I could see in the river was story. I saw the stories of my ancestors.

My mother's story, her mother's story. I felt them bursting like a dam in my bloodstream. I felt my own story start to swell up like a flood in me. I had been silent for so long it nearly drowned me.

The Crucible

We were going to go to a place called the Gold Coast in Australia. I spent mornings looking at photos online of white-sand beaches, turquoise waters, and the Great Barrier Reef. Schools of fish floated in crystal waters, like something you'd see in a dentist's fish tank, a real dentist, not the bleak waiting room of Indian Health Services. These fish were fancy. I imagined myself suspended in water, weightless against a backdrop of tropical fish, a shimmering rainbow of scales and fins. I had given up on my idea of gloomy coastlines and moody nights of rain for sunshine and sea turtles. It felt appropriate. I was struggling against my sadness and nightmares. A place like the Gold Coast sounded like medicine.

Brandon had gotten the okay from his bandmates, and because a wealthy friend of his family gifted us two thousand dollars to put toward a honeymoon fund, it was possible now. I would join him on the tour in Australia, then we would stay an extra ten days to have a proper honeymoon. The trip was a week out.

"Look, we can fly to New Zealand," I beamed up at him from my spot on our couch, surrounded by piles of wedding presents still unwrapped. "We can see the Shire!" He just sighed and stomped into the kitchen, seemingly annoyed or frustrated by my trip planning. He had been acting strange for weeks.

I followed him into our kitchen.

Something horrible tugged at my insides. I was tense and adrenalized. My throat felt raw when I swallowed, like I might cry, right there next to the French press. My body knew something the rest of me didn't. Brandon just stood silently looking at the hardwood floor.

"I'm going to the beach." I said it cold and calm. I had had enough. "I'm going to go for a swim. Take this time to figure out how to tell me whatever it is you need to say."

On the short drive through our neighborhood I tried to brace myself for whatever might be coming. Ever since my book project and my memories started, we had been having a hard time. I blamed myself. I had thrown myself into the past so intensely and so fully that whatever was left of me seemed like a pale imitation. Did he feel like he married a stranger? Was he meeting all of my ghosts at once? Was it too much for him? I tried to calm down. Maybe he was just stressed about the tour.

I arrived at Lake Washington and walked straight into the water, barely stopping to drop my bag and clothes against a pile of driftwood. The water held me up like hands, and my skin warmed in the morning sun. Weightless, I felt at peace. The women of my family get their power from water, that's what I have been told. Their songs come to them, and they feel them most next to rivers, lakes, and oceans. I tried to quiet myself and listen. I heard the gentle waves pushing against the stones onshore. I heard the breeze rustling lightly through the trees. I heard kids playing and dogs barking, a car stereo in the distance. I heard nothing within me that spoke of strength. The only thing I heard was that familiar nagging voice, the one that had been with me since childhood, reminding me that I was lost and alone. As my body floated along the surface, tears slid down my cheeks.

As I pulled on my clothes, I looked out at the boats on Lake Washington. I wondered again why Comptia had decided to marry the Scottish sea captain. Did he promise her something? Gold? Security? Was it safety he offered? The captain was rumored to have been a pirate. In one of my mom's documents there is a story about Capt. James Johnson's buried treasure. My ancestor married a pirate in a settlement that would eventually become Astoria, Oregon, the setting for the movie *The Goonies*. How appropriate. The Goonies are a group of misfit teens in the small coastal town, who embark on a treasure hunt that leads them on a wild ride through sea caves and caverns, where they outsmart criminals and hundred-year-old booby traps. The Goonies are obsessed with finding the treacherous pirate One-Eyed Willy and his hidden treasure, so they set out on their quest with only a torn piece of a map to guide them. In a way, I had my own piece of map. The papers, clippings, and letters were my clues, but I wasn't looking for buried treasure. I wanted answers. Why had Comptia said yes? Was she afraid? Or was she in love? Goonies never say "die"—that's their motto. But Goonies never had to say "colonize." Goonies never had to say "smallpox." It wasn't so straightforward for Comptia. Back at the house, I was damp from the lake and worried. I sat on the couch considering a sky-blue cooking pot with a French name. Why had we even put that on our registry? I didn't cook.

Brandon came into the room and sat down.

"What is it?" I asked, ready for answers. "What is going on? Is it about the tour? Just talk to me." He sighed and shifted uncomfortably. Then his body language changed. He steadied himself. Sturdy and hard, he shifted into something colder.

"It is about Australia. You're not . . . going . . . You

can't go. I wasn't able to make it work." His hardness soft-ened. He seemed flustered now, panicked. As he began to explain how he had lied to me months earlier, when I first learned of the Australian tour, I felt dizzy. I felt like I might throw up. My ears started to ring. He had told me the band was being flown out, that the tickets had been paid for. I remembered this, because it was one of the reasons for choosing the tour over our honeymoon. I had been told there was no way to postpone, because the tickets had been paid for. The money, the gift we had received to take our own trip, was supposed to buy my ticket to Australia. That was the plan. But he had used the money to buy his own ticket, without me. His voice shook a little when he said "without you." Some innate obligation to comfort him overwhelmed me. I wanted to put an arm around him or a hand on his shoulder, but I remained still, my limbs tingling, starting with the tips of my fingers. *Needles and pins.* With a Ramones song now stupidly in my head, the tingling crawled up my arms to my shoulders and chest, then up my neck and to my sun-kissed cheeks. I felt the warmth of the day snuffed out like a candle.

I deserve this. The words briefly looped in my head. *I deserve this*, because I don't deserve his love, his attention, his time. I brought my hands to my face and cried into them. *This is because you're broken.* Closing my eyes, I saw the trailer in the woods, the amber streaks of rust running down the metal siding. I saw a mess of brown curls and a dirty face. I saw a child alone next to a pile of trash, then in the woods, then next to a fire. I squeezed my face harder in the palms of my hands. I tried to strangle whatever was happening to me. Then a new voice came. A really pissed-off voice. All I could hear was screaming. Things like *you lied, you tricked me, you fucking stole it for yourself, you're greedy, you're selfish, you don't love me* echoed in my ears. They bounced off the silver and lace-printed wrapping paper that covered all the boxes around us. The words reverberated off the gifts and the bottles of champagne and the piles of cards reading "Congratulations." I heard them shrill and angry: *You knew. You fucking knew and you lied to me. You tricked me.* Then I saw four walls and a dirt floor, I saw through a single window into a great big house, a house I wasn't allowed to live in. *You tricked me. You lied.* Then I realized that the words were coming from my own mouth. I had been yelling them out loud, screaming until I couldn't scream anymore. I had screamed myself into exhaustion.

If I slept at the house at all that week, I did so in my writing studio. The days went slow and with hardly any pulse. I felt drugged, turned into something hollow. I don't remember much, until the day he left. He looked handsome. His dark hair, tight black pants, leather jacket, and a guitar slung over his shoulder. People always look the most beautiful as they're walking out the door. All throughout the wedding planning, the dress fittings, the cakes, the seating arrangements, the endless organizing, he had been planning a tour that wouldn't include me.

"I'm sorry," he said before he disappeared out the front door and into a white van that would take him to the airport where he would board a plane that would take him to Australia. "I made the wrong choice. I put the band ahead of you. I know that I messed up."

I watched him go, stunned into a silence I had not expected. He walked out the door, leaving me in the debris of our recent celebration. I sat alone on the couch for hours, looking around our home, my so-called permanent place.

—

My great-grandmother married her first husband when she was just a teenager. She had traveled up and down the Skagit River her entire childhood, and after attending the Tulalip Indian Boarding School, she had graduated and learned the skills necessary to be a maid in white households. Not wanting to simply return to her parents' home after graduation, she decided to travel with a friend to the southwest coast of Washington, to Quinault. There she met Percy Woodcock and, after only a handful of dates, married him.

My great-grandmother wanted her own life, her

own home. Her new husband, a skilled carpenter, built her a café. She was a hard worker. She ran the restaurant as a new wife and a young mother. In the 1930s she was an educated native woman, a teenager, not working in a white household as a maid but running her own business.

There is a way that memory lives in our bodies, imprints us with feeling. When I was in my early twenties, Brandon and I went on a date to the coast. We hiked the rain-swept forests and climbed around the rocky shoreline. While rounding a corner of the mossy, overgrown trail, I was suddenly overcome with a sense of familiarity. Some might call it déjà vu, that strange sensation of an implanted memory. But what I felt, I recognized in my bones, in my very core. I was shaken. I kept walking down the trail until it opened up to a dark wet expanse of sand. The gray beach was moody. The waves crawled up the shore leaving trembling wisps of sea-foam. Though it was cold I removed my shoes in the afternoon drizzle and stepped toward the ocean. The wind picked up and the waves grew taller. Beyond the breakers I could see waves climbing upward, as the ocean swelled in the promise of an oncoming storm.

"We should go," Brandon said behind me, but I took another step into the water. Then another. I stood there, held by the vast ocean. In its grip I looked out, unable to see the horizon. The storm brought the sky down into the water, in a running of colors, blue, gray, and violet. His hand on mine snapped me out of my trance and I returned to the beach, the wet sand, and my date. Later I told my mom about my experience and she sighed.

"I never told you about this," she started, "but your great-grandmother had one of the darkest moments of her life while she lived in Quinault." I knew the version of my namesake's history I had always been told, the one of my great-grandmother beating the odds as a young native woman, finding her own way, her own happiness, a marriage, a business, children, but there was a part that I had not heard.

When my great-grandmother lived in Quinault her business was ransacked, looted. The windows were busted out, broken glass everywhere, and she had been robbed. It wasn't that her husband couldn't fix it. He was a carpenter; he could have fixed it for her. But the robbery shook her more because it had happened within her own community, a place she was learning to call home.

Soon after the robbery, her youngest child, her three-year-old son Denny, came down with an unexpected fever. Meningitis can be cured these days. But in the 1930s, the infection was fatal. Her son left this world quickly and left her brokenhearted.

My great-grandmother walked the trail down to the shore. She stood, a young woman against the waves, staring out at the roaring ocean. "I wanted to walk out into the water and drown," she told my mother years ago. "My heart was broken."

Her carpenter husband could not fix it. No matter how much he may have wanted to, he could not rebuild what was lost. He could not join her in her heartbreak. So she left. Unable to live the life she wanted to with him, she packed up her things and her remaining children and went back up north. She traveled back to the Skagit River to live with her mother. Just like that, she left him.

The day Brandon left for Australia, I went to a show with my friend Malari, then we went to a bar and then another. I tried to postpone as long as I could walking back through the door and into my phantom home. Looking at the framed photos of Brandon and me on the walls and the photo-booth strips and ticket stubs on the fridge made me feel like I was behind a veil, a specter forced to haunt her own life. But I had to go back. It was expected of me. We had been joined beneath the blanket. In the eyes of my ancestors we were married, spiritually.

"I don't even know how to use this," I said as I nearly tripped over the sky-blue ceramic pot. I stumbled over the pile of wedding gifts in the living room and dropped into the sofa with my phone in hand. The screen glowed with the current ticket prices to Morocco. For $1,400 I could fly to North Africa. Malari masterfully confiscated my phone. "Maybe you shouldn't be trying to fly to Morocco after cocktails."

She wasn't wrong. Least of all because I didn't have money to go to Morocco. I just knew I wanted to leave.

I kicked the beautiful ceramic pot at my feet. "What does Le Creuset even mean, you know? Besides fancy kitchen shit white women use to bake their Pinterest masterpieces in."

"I think it means something in French," Malari laughed and shrugged, "right?"

"You're right." I stared at the empty pot in front of me. "It means 'crucible.'"

Comptia Koholowish

First, she watched them lose their appetite. One by one the people in her family came down with a fever. They began to vomit. They began to change. It started with their mouths, sores and bumps spreading from where they spoke. Then a rash covered their limbs, followed by boils. Their blistering bodies seemed to fill with a poison. Comptia was nine when she watched smallpox devour her people.

In order to survive, she left. She knew the trails and waterways. She was able to get far away from the nothing that was left of her village. Comptia Koholowish survived.

When she met Capt. James Johnson of the Hudson Bay Trading Company she was twenty years old. He was a Scottish sea captain who had sailed from Shetland. By that time Comptia was used to meeting captains.

Coast Salish people believe we are all connected to the land we come from and are as such identified by the land: Chinook, Quinault, Skagit, or Swinomish, for example. When the first white people arrived on ships, the Coast Salish asked where they came from and they responded with the word "Boston," which became "Pastad" in the first peoples' language. "Pastad" became the word for all white people. Comptia met many of the Pastads. They had come when she was young. They built forts and set up trade routes. They traded furs, they traded salted salmon. What Comptia used to recognize as the land she came from was now the Astoria Trading Post. Then the Hudson Bay Trading Company arrived. Then there were many Pastads. Priests arrived. They built churches and began baptizing and naming the people.

Comptia knew her world was changing. She watched it shift and grow. Buildings climbed up into the sky, and more ships came. Comptia Koholowish knew that in order to survive she, too, would have to change, so when Capt. James Johnson asked her to marry him, she said yes. But her survival came with a price. She lost her name. Comptia Koholowish became Mrs. Jane Johnson.

A Good Wife

"You had a blanket-wrapping ceremony." My mom's eyes
leveled over her latte, right into mine. Her tone was serious. I poked at my pastry. "You have to give it a year."
Brandon was still in Australia, emailing me, telling me
he made a mistake, telling me he loved me. The words
stung, reminding me of his choice, of his absence. An
empty house only made things worse. Our housemates
had moved out and in their place was a living room
entombing the great pile of unwrapped wedding gifts.
They greeted me each morning, a sad shrine to the life I
thought we wanted. I had to get out, so I moved into our
friend Rob's apartment for the month. He was in Berlin
and needed someone to look after his place.

———

The day I found out about the Australian tour I drove an hour north. I showed up on Richard's doorstep panicked. "I messed up, didn't I? I thought I was doing the right thing. You said to do the right thing." He sighed and looked down at me from his doorway, his gentle green eyes heavy with sadness. Richard's small frame and delicate face gave him the appearance of a fawn, something that would never, could never, hurt me. He invited me in, made me a small bed on his floor out of a pile of blankets and let me cry as we shared a bottle of wine and listened to the albums we loved as teenagers. I stayed for days. He took me to the gallery where he worked, and I watched him frame art and we talked until dawn. We walked along the banks of the Skagit River and drank dark beers and played card games. I was putting the hard parts of myself to sleep and traveling back in time. As children we had been careful and innocent. Being with him felt like picking up where we left off. Maybe there was a chance for us still. Maybe coming back up north was where I needed to be. Maybe this had always been my home.

"I can't be the thing that takes you away from your marriage," he told me before I returned to Seattle. "If you and Brandon can work it out and be happy, then you need to stay and be happy. I want that, for both of you."

I could see he wanted more. But he was too good, too

careful, and too caring to pursue it. The truth is I was not a good wife. I was trying to be, yet I drove back north to see Richard once, then twice a week. I let myself fall back in time with him. An emotional affair seems more innocent than a physical one, but it's far more dangerous.

Richard and I took a trip to the Swinomish Reservation. I found the trailer I once called home. I wanted to see the last place that had felt safe to me, before nothing would again. Nearly missing the driveway, I had to back up and turn off the road into the brush. It was unrecognizable. Blackberry bushes climbed the rusted walls of the trailer, encasing my childhood home in thorns, like some dark fairy-tale spell. A tree branch had crashed through the living room window. Vines covered the tin rooftop, and the shed where we stacked firewood was swallowed by sword ferns. Around the property old appliances sank into the mud. Two abandoned fireworks stands stood on either side of the trailer, and a garbage heap rose up almost as tall the cedar trees behind it. *This is where I lived.*

When we moved here, it was with plans to build a permanent home. Instead, we lived without power, without running water, we shit in a portable toilet, and we showered at a nearby campground.

Walking the grounds was like walking through time. I saw the stump where my sister and I had buried over a dozen tubes of Lip Smacker lip gloss. Ashamed after shoplifting from the only drugstore in town, we agreed to bury our looted makeup behind a massive tree stump. I touched the damp earth with my hand and smiled. Somewhere in the dirt was a pile of our favorite lip gloss flavors: cherry vanilla, Dr. Pepper, and kiwi strawberry. I looked up to the driveway. Across the street and through the trees lived the neighbor who assaulted me when I was ten. He was forty.

We'd had to leave the trailer after that. We lived in basements and on friends' couches. We lived in the attic of the Swinomish Tribal Church. I don't think I really considered the word "homeless" until I saw my bags in the back of our Pinto, my roll-out mattress in the dark room of that church.

When we moved into the church, I became acquainted with shame. On the bus rides home from school, I shrank down into the brown, vinyl seat until I was sure no one could see me. Shame was the feeling that stirred when I knew the bus was approaching my new stop. Walking up the street and taking a left led into the village. Walking down the street led to the Swinomish Community Center, where kids could play basketball in the gym. Dead ahead was the Swinomish church, my new home. I learned to wait, to fumble with my backpack or pretend to tie my shoes. Waiting until the other kids disappeared and the bus pulled away.

One afternoon, after the usual charade, I passed the chapel and the commissary kitchen and made my way up the carpeted stairs to the little space my family occupied. I did homework and watched a movie on the TV used for community gatherings. That night, my parents brought home Chinese food. We didn't often cook meals while living in the church. Most of our dinners were either the quick, drive-through kind, things wrapped in paper, or frozen. The Chinese food felt decadent.

I finished my sweet-and-sour chicken and rice and went to bed feeling full. I woke a few hours later with my stomach in knots. My body twisted in pain as I tossed and turned on my roll-out mattress, feeling the bile rise from my stomach into my throat. I remember not wanting to wake my parents and being afraid of the dark. I mustered the courage to traverse the unlit landscape of the church. Feeling my way through the halls, I found the staircase and inched my way down to the main floor and past the chapel, its rows of pews, wooden and militant in the dark. The carvings of the saints eyed me. When I reached the bathroom I flicked on the light, crawled to a stall, and threw up violently. Tears streamed down my face as I hurled the neon-red remnants of chicken and the flaky paper skin of fortune cookies into the toilet. Wrapping my small body around the porcelain and shaking on the tiles, I cried.

I remember hating the food, as it overwhelmed me in the dark, as it made me sick. I hated the red-and-white paper boxes it came in, the disposable wooden chopsticks, the cardboard flat it was stacked in. I hated my mom for bringing it to us, for not being able to cook a meal with pots and pans, with greens on the side that she would scold me for not eating. I hated our disposable picnics, without a long table and chairs and salt and pepper shakers and glasses of milk, like normal families. I hated that I had brought us here, to the church. I felt shame rise up in me. It came foaming out of my mouth and spewing into the toilet. This wasn't a home. This wasn't where I belonged. This wasn't how it was supposed to be.

—

We passed the church on our way to the trailer. Across the street through the trees stood the longhouse, over two hundred feet of wooden planks that housed the winter ceremonies. When we drove past it, I could almost hear the faint sounds of drumming.

I visited the trailer hoping to uncover something, but it just stood before me, rotting and empty. I climbed into the decaying doorway. The mirror in the bathroom was cracked and covered in mildew, reflecting a distorted version of myself back at me. I stepped carefully down the narrow hallway, looking out for the places where the floor had rotted away. I passed my bedroom. The walls had yellowed and were covered with spots of mold. The place where my twin bed had been was blanketed in thick moss, and leaves littered the floor. Roots coiled the walls, thick and snakelike.

Then I came to the living room, a space that seemed more like a forest than a home. Ferns and small trees sprouted from surfaces. Giant holes in the rooftop let the daylight in in warm yellow beams. There were broken shelves covered in dirt and plants, and rot-spotted walls. I saw the black wood stove in the center of the room, the only thing still clinging to its structural integrity. I looked at it and immediately thought of Christmas morning. I turned the corner and came into what used to be the kitchen. I saw boxes of board games mildewing in a pile in the corner. Stacks of rusted pots littered the faded countertops. I made crafts in this room as a kid. There is a video of me counting to ten in Lushootseed on my fingers here. I bent down and picked up a damp photo album. Inside were the pictures of my aunt and uncle and their children. They were the last people to live here and last I heard had been caught selling pills on the reservation. They spent time in jail and in rehab and left this place abandoned. This is what abandonment looked like. I dropped the old album to the ground in a dull thud and circled the room. When I came to the stove, my eyes stayed on the charred wiring just above the stovetop. The evidence of a fry bread recipe gone wrong. The fires my mom used to set while trying to make fry bread terrified us as kids, but they happened so frequently that they eventually became a source of amusement. The burnt wires and blackened spots up the wall filled me with a sort of homesickness. It couldn't have been easy for them, my young parents and their five kids crammed into this temporary home. Sunlight came in through what remained of the mud-caked windowpane. I traced a heart on the glass with my fingertips and cried in the ruins of my kitchen.

I drove back to the city wondering what a permanent home might look like. Maybe I wouldn't even recognize it. Reservations should not have been a permanent home. Like trailers, like campgrounds, like prisons or hospitals, they felt temporary, like some place you go between places. I realized I wasn't sure what permanence looked like, because we weren't meant to survive. My family, my tribe, my ancestors, we were something temporary to the settlers. Something that would eventually go away. Whether by disease or alcohol or poverty, our genocide was inevitable to them. I looked at the smoke pluming from the metal chimneys of the small reservation houses along the highway. But here we were, existing in our impermanent homes.

———

I pulled over along a road that curved against the water. I was angry at Brandon. In my fist I held the rose-gold wedding ring he'd given me and cried. I opened my hand and it sparkled in the daylight. Rings are supposed to be permanent, are supposed to represent forever, and here I was on the side of a rural reservation highway, lost. I thought of throwing it into the bay. Instead, I shoved it back into my pocket, unable to wear it or hurl it into the waves.

Back in Seattle, seated at a small table in a local café, my mom's fingers drummed quietly against the table as I confessed how badly I wanted to leave. "Take your time," her voice softened, but she was still short. "Stay at your friend's if you need to, but consider hearing him out when he gets home." I sighed and stared into my empty mug, then looked around the café. People around us chatted and worked on laptops like their lives were perfectly intact. "The blanket-wrapping ceremony is serious. Give it a year. You can stick it out."

My mom wanted me to stay, to be a good wife. I had spent weeks angry, I had spent weeks falling back in love with my childhood sweetheart, but I wanted to try. I wanted to be a good wife.

Breath

My first poem was published two days before Brandon got back from Australia. I was still camping out at Rob's house and found out about the publication over morning coffee in his sunlit breakfast nook. I loved living in the old brick apartment building. The art was not mine. The plants were not mine, neither were the sheets, the chairs, the flat-screen TV, or this little nook where I spent my mornings. In his apartment I could listen to records, make coffee, make ramen, and drink red wine out of glasses that weren't wedding gifts. In his apartment I could be someone who never wanted to get married. When I received the news about the poem, I felt a small shiver, something like hope, shake my body, uneasy but not unwelcome. Maybe I was going to be okay.

Brandon showed up on the doorstep with white roses the day after he flew in from Australia. "They're congratulatory flowers," he said as we hugged, "for getting published." I appreciated the disclaimer. I hated apology flowers. He stayed for dinner. We made soup and drank dark ale and watched movies on the couch. It felt okay to be with him in neutral territory.

A week later I was packing my bags to move back home. I wanted to be ready for a home. I still texted Richard daily, though. I rationalized that this was okay because we had reconnected in such a deep way that the friendship felt ingrained in me. Something as natural and as necessary as breathing. When I'd see him, it was still innocent, still childlike. I believed him when he said, "Try to be happy with Brandon, it's what's right." It felt like unconditional love. It also felt like something I couldn't let go of.

Brandon and I eased back into occupying space. I was still jumpy and on edge. My impulse to run, to be that girl who slept in bowling alleys and unfinished buildings, still crept up. She threatened everything. I looked at Brandon and couldn't help seeing a liar. He had become someone unsafe. He tried hard to fight against that role by being sweet, attentive, and listening. He even surprised me in a big way by asking me to be in a band with him.

I smiled as we lay sprawled out in my writing studio. I had been writing all day, and after dinner we put on records and lounged in the small space. He showed me a recording of a new project he was working on.

"We need someone to sing," he said. He knew I desperately wanted to sing in a band. Ever since I had curled my teenage body along the yellow linoleum of a bathroom reading the liner notes and lyric sheets of Bikini Kill's *Pussy Whipped*, I had wanted badly to sing in a band. I knew it the first time I heard Kathleen Hanna's girl-like voice scream lyrics about date rape and the aftermath of assault, of being betrayed by a boy who had claimed to be a friend. I played "Star Bellied Boy" on repeat in our small bathroom. I pressed play and rewind. Play and rewind in a trance. I had never heard a song about assault before, let alone one that seemed to mirror my own. To hear her singsong voice go into a shrieking, guttural scream felt like being in the presence of power, which I wanted so badly to possess. I knew the night I wandered into my first basement punk show in the U District in Seattle. I went alone, nervous and feeling misfit. When I heard Laura Jane Grace scream into the mic to a room erupting in singing and dancing, I knew I had wandered into a world I wanted to be a part of. All of my friends were in bands. The people I fell in love with were in bands. But never me. I'd help out at shows, sell merch, hang out. But it was never me onstage. Over the early years of our relationship, my desire to sing would come up and I'd ask Brandon to give me a shot. I even did my very best version of Joan Jett's "I Hate Myself for Loving You" in a drunken karaoke attempt to win him over. But he always told me the same thing. He had strong reservations against any kind of collaboration with a partner. I had been asking for years. He always told me no. Not while we were dating, not while I was his girlfriend, and not now that I was his wife.

But as our marriage felt threatened, as it began to unravel and as I felt farther and farther away from him, he attempted to appease me with a last-ditch effort. I didn't know that when he came to me with that recording. All I knew was that the teenager that was somewhere still in me was exploding with the anticipation of her punk rock dreams coming true.

"Maybe we could try it?" he shrugged. "You are a poet. Maybe you'd be good at writing lyrics." He left me that night in the studio with the recording. "Just listen to it, see what it says to you, put some cool words to it." I listened to the sounds of the instruments and closed my eyes. I saw women in red.

The next morning over coffee I showed Brandon my lyrics. He nodded in approval. "This is really good." I beamed. A small hope took seed and I let the idea that we would do something beautiful together bloom.

—

I still struggled with flashbacks and PTSD. Episodes would sneak up on me on the train, in shopping centers, even while I slept. One night I woke in a panic. I felt lost, my surroundings unrecognizable. My heart pounded in my chest and I was sure I was having a heart attack. It was just another nightmare, but I was irrational with fear and my body shook in the muscle memory of someone violating it. To calm myself I turned on the TV. Its light flickering against the shadows, its muffled sounds breaking the silence, pushed the panic into the background. I had been doing this a lot, so often that Brandon became increasingly frustrated with me. I scrolled through Netflix and settled on Brandon Lee's *The Crow.* I wanted to drift off to visions of a ghost in leather pants jumping over rooftops, playing guitar, and avenging his murdered beloved. The movies worked some nights. Not this night. Brandon woke in a fit of anger. He tossed and turned and scolded me about his early work morning. He shoved his pillow over his head, trying to block out the noise, before finally demanding I turn it off. Unable to sleep in the silent blackness of our bedroom, I spent the night on the couch—something else that was becoming a habit. On nights like these I'd look around the dark of our living room and take inventory. Things started to feel less and less like home. I would text Richard. I would ask if he was up. Each time I did this I hated myself for the comfort it brought me. The glow of my phone like a night-light brought stories of our childhood into the room. Good memories of walking the streets of our small town, listening to mixtapes, and talking about comic books and movies. I wanted to fall into those stories and stay there. Eventually I'd drift off to sleep.

Brandon and I sat in my car following a date night at my favorite pizza spot in Seattle that had gone like so many previous attempts: uneasy and gentle, at first, like traversing a minefield, then explosive. My phone sat between us on the console. It lit up with a message from Richard: "I love you too." Brandon saw it and was angry. He slammed his hands against the steering wheel. "Are you fucking kidding me, Sasha?" Something like shame caught in the back of my throat. Unable to explain myself, all I could say was "I do love him. But I love you too." He was losing me, and he could feel it. What terrified me was that I felt like I was losing my safe place, my linoleum, and myself.

—

Leaving my body wasn't unknown to me. I had learned to disassociate when I was ten as a defense tactic. It wasn't an ability I was consciously aware of. It would just sort of happen. A fog would cloud my brain, and I'd slip down into myself to someplace safe. It was as involuntary as breathing. It was reflex. But when the strange phenomenon came back into my life as an adult, I wasn't really prepared.

It had been a little over a year since the Australian tour. Brandon and I had been trying to move past it, but I grew colder as the months went by. I sank deep down into myself. I drove up north more frequently. I rekindled a deep relationship with my fourteen-year-old self, convinced that if I could tap into the past I could save myself from drowning in memory in the present. I retraced her steps, returning again and again to the trailer. Things only got worse. Brandon tried to reassure me. "I'm here," he kept telling me. "You've got to move past this." So I tried. He was also trying, trying to regain my trust, trying to right the wrong of abandoning me. He presented me with a trip to Ireland. His band was going on tour again, in Europe, and this time he tried to choose me as much as he could. He chose both, convinced he could balance a trip with me and his tour, starting the trip together in Dublin and eventually meeting up with the band. I agreed to go to Ireland with him, believing that if we could recreate the fantasy of rainy nights next to a fire and crashing ocean waves, we could have a chance.

The first time I fainted I was walking across the parking lot outside a market in Dublin. I collapsed onto the concrete and Brandon rushed to me, bringing me to my feet and offering me my inhaler. I took two puffs. My body quaked with tremors, like the medication somehow aggravated my condition rather than helped my breath return. Back in the hotel that night I curled my body along the window as Brandon slept. I looked down at the city below, still bustling with the drunken noises of nightlife. We decided the attack was a result of my asthma, that perhaps the travel had been a trigger. I looked at my plastic inhaler, then back out to the lively streets of Dublin, unconvinced the small plastic rescue inhaler would truly save me.

After two weeks in Ireland, we joined his band in Italy. The fainting continued as we traveled in the van across Europe. I kept it to myself when I could. I shrank down into the back of the van. I tried to make myself invisible. I tried to make myself useful. I sold merch, loaded gear, and fought against anxiety. I took care of the asthma attacks when I could. In Slovenia after helping unload the van and while the band set up in the venue, I grabbed my bag and took off into the lamplit village. Brandon worried about me going alone, but I assured him I would be fine. I wanted a bed and a bath and an evening to myself. I needed a break from smoke-filled venues, rowdy crowds, and loud guitars.

That night I walked the cobblestoned pathways along the river. Great stone statues of dragons and gargoyles looked over me as I made my way through the narrow roads. The village made me think of Dracula, specifically Gary Oldman in *Bram Stoker's Dracula*. I thought about sex and candles. I missed romance. I missed intimacy. I ate a salad and a slice of pizza by the water. I drank a glass of red wine. On my way to the inn, I stumbled upon a beautiful marble fountain in the middle of a dark square. Illuminated by a single streetlamp, the fountain looked dark and ominous. I climbed the steps and sat on the ledge. Figures of sea maidens and merfolk glowed against the shadows. Sitting at the fountain I let the fear of whatever was happening to me—breathlessness, blackouts, loss of consciousness—find me. I sat by the fountain in the moonlit plaza and wept, alone and so far from home. Along with the fear, a certainty crept in. I was not where I needed to be, but wherever I was supposed to be was unknown.

The tour went on. Fainting came in and out. I was juggling graduate work and selling the band's merch in loud DIY punk bars and venues. In Prague I sat posted at the bar for hours wrapping up an essay before a midnight deadline, then drank a glass of absinthe and walked the Charles Bridge. In England I lost my spot in the van. The guys had invited a friend from Greece to join in on the last leg of the tour, and the week he was to join them, the van they were driving broke down. They got a new van, but it had one seat fewer.

The plan was that I would do some traveling on my own. Spend time in Berlin and Hamburg, before meeting back up with the band in London. I wasn't afraid of traveling alone, but I was afraid of losing my breath. I was afraid of fainting on my own. Still I ventured into train stations and unknown cities independently. I eventually made it to King's Cross Station in downtown London, the rendezvous spot, and waited. And waited. The van never came. Finally I got a message from Brandon explaining the guys wanted to stop in Camden Town to visit a famous record shop. He had no control over this, he explained. I had ridden a train and a bus from Bristol to make it to this meeting place. I was sick and I was terrified of fainting. A relentless cough had settled in my chest, and each day the rumbling wheeze in my lungs became worse. I just sighed and offered to wait it out, but when he said they were stuck in bad traffic I knew they weren't going to pick me up. He sent me a pin of the warehouse they were playing in. I'd have to meet them at the venue.

—

Comptia was only nine years old when she first encountered the flu that would nearly destroy the Chinook people. The disease spread quickly, and she watched as one by one her family succumbed. There is no known record of the years between the recorded smallpox epidemic and her marriage to Capt. James Johnson. Years Comptia spent alone, working, surviving, and growing into the young woman that would eventually marry one of the settlers whose arrival had led to her village's erasure. I learned the captain was a pirate and a bootlegger, selling distilled spirits to the few survivors of Comptia's tribe. As I traveled alone, ill with bronchitis, I wondered if the captain ever cared for her in sickness. Did he bring her tea and warm broth? Did he bring her extra blankets? I changed trains three times and rode to the end of the line. Then I walked. I walked for hours, past giant housing complexes and shopping centers. The boroughs gave way to enormous warehouses and factories, and I worried about what might happen to me if I were to drop to the ground and faint out here alone. When I finally arrived at the collective warehouse space where the show was booked, a volunteer showed me to the kitchen. There I made a cup of peppermint tea before collapsing onto a couch. That night I curled up on a sofa during a rowdy afterparty. I coughed my body into spasms and tried to sleep. I woke to see the silhouette of a man carefully arranging blankets over me. For the first time in days I felt nurtured, cared for. Groggy from cough syrup I wanted to reach up, to pull him close, and whisper *I love you*, but when I blinked his face into view, the man caring for me wasn't my husband. He was a complete stranger, the lead singer from one of the touring bands. Brandon was two rooms over, beer in hand, surrounded by bandmates and laughter. The stranger seemed to notice my confusion, asked if I needed anything, then smiled sympathetically before returning to the party. To this day whenever his band comes on the overhead at a punk venue or bar, I close my eyes in gratitude and remember his face. The tour continued on to Paris, where I left to stay with friends as the band drove on to Switzerland. My bronchitis turned into walking pneumonia, and when I returned to the States I was hospitalized and put on antibiotics.

—

Back home, I became withdrawn. I sank deeper into sadness. I tried to be present. We threw dinner parties and went to shows, but I was falling. One night as we sat around a fire with friends, I remembered the song I had worked on. A tiny spark lit up in me. I asked Brandon about the project, I wanted to know how it was going, if he had any more recordings he wanted me to hear. Maybe I could practice writing lyrics again.

"Oh, we decided to go with Anne." He said it plainly, like it wouldn't come as a shock to me, like it wouldn't hurt my heart. I felt something shut down in me that night. Our friend Anne was indeed a gifted vocalist. She had a strong presence and a powerful voice. It's not that I didn't know she'd be a better fit than me. I just wanted to feel chosen by him, my partner. I had imagined us together, him playing guitar, me singing. I imagined us traveling together, a dark and romantic musical duo. I imagined us not with his band but as equals.

The fainting became more frequent after that. Without warning I would lose my breath completely. Each time, I thought I would die. I was thirty-three years old and wearing heart monitors for the fainting. Doctors tracked my every heartbeat for thirty days. They did an ultrasound of my heart, a chest X-ray. They hooked me up to machines while I ran on a treadmill and did multiple EKG tests. The tests were inconclusive; the doctors just told me to keep an eye on my asthma and to come back if the fainting didn't stop.

The day it became really bad we were driving across Tacoma with my parents. We had gone to lunch, and my parents were showing us around the city. The city had a bleak, Pacific Northwest kind of charm. "Maybe Brandon and you could move down here someday," my mom said, sounding hopeful. My other grandmother, my dad's mom, was selling her house to move back up north. I remembered the house from when I was a kid, coming to big family gatherings and barbecues. Somewhere between the restaurant and the stretch of road leading toward the Tacoma Narrows Bridge, I lost my breath. I puffed on my inhaler. I felt faint. My mom was sitting in the back seat with me, and the look on her face when I showed her my left hand reassured me that it was not my imagination. My hand was pale, white, drained of color. Then it turned blue. The blue traveled up my wrist and forearm. My left arm was cold to the touch and numb. I hadn't taken a breath for several minutes. My chest tightened. I looked at my mom looking back at me and then everything went dark.

When I came to, the doctors were taking my vitals. I felt the squeeze of the machine that read my blood pressure, different faces coming in and out of view. I heard the words "hypertensive crisis." None of it made sense. They lay me down in a hospital bed. Different people came in and out asking my mom and Brandon questions. I felt the prick of a needle in my arm, then another as they gave me fluids. They took an EKG and sent me home with a packet on severe asthma and panic attacks. I rode home in a veil of medication. My senses dulled, my heart beat slow and sleepy.

—

In the documents of our family's lineage, there is no known cause for Comptia's death. Just that she died young, unexpectedly at thirty-five years of age. The oral histories of who she was, where she came from, and that she was her family's sole survivor of the smallpox epidemic had been passed down by the women in my family, but all we knew about her death was that it happened in her thirties, seemingly for no reason at all.

I lived in fear of my own body after my trip to the hospital. They said an asthma attack coupled with a panic attack caused a lack of oxygen, which is why my arm turned blue. They said I was suffocating. They were right in more ways than one. Maybe it was my heart. Maybe it was Comptia's heart. Maybe Comptia died of a broken heart and maybe I would too.

But I didn't want to die. I wanted to be okay, to be better. So I lived in the house, busied myself with graduate school work. I tried to ignore whatever was happening inside my body. I was still bitter about Australia, the European tour, and now losing the chance to be in a band with Brandon. Driving home from a show on a stormy Seattle night, we fought. I was still leaving all the time, spending time away from home, from him. I was being unfair—he wasn't wrong. But I was angry and scared and trying to hold on to myself. I buried my tear-streaked face in my hands.

"You don't know what this is like!" I screamed at him as the rain beat against the windshield. "Not knowing if you're just gonna drop to the floor, faint for no reason. The nightmares. The flashbacks. Seeing strangers on the train turn into my rapist. Seeing *you* turn into my rapist." I began to cough and wheeze.

"Because you won't let me understand!" he fired back. "Ever since you started writing this stupid book, since you went to the trailer. All you do is hang out with Richard. You're not even dealing with your shit. You've been seeing a PTSD counselor for months! It hasn't done anything! You're not even trying!" The truck pulled into our driveway and I stepped out into the wet night.

"I am trying! I try every day that I stay here. Every day that I faint, or black out, or have a flashback. I'm trying!" I yelled over the traffic and rain.

"How long are you gonna let your trauma be your entire life!?"

At this there was a long, dark silence. I stared him down, unblinking in the downpour.

The wounds I carried inside my body, the aftermath of historical trauma, of sexual assault, the generations of ancestors that came before me who had faced violence, disease, and genocide, were distilled down into something small, reduced. He presented my entire history, my identity, my feelings of distrust and displacement as some kind of personality tic, a bad habit, like biting your nails or chewing your food too loudly. I felt some invisible force slam into my gut, and it knocked the wind out of me. I blinked and saw a sea of red. It happened fast. I had never hit a partner in my life, outside of waking from a flashback and pushing against a lover, defensive and terrified. It was never like this, never on purpose. My hand snapped back and struck his cheek in a wet slap that left my palm stinging. Immediately ashamed, I covered my mouth.

"I'm so sorry!" I apologized through my fingers and the anger I still felt. It had been a horrible thing for him to say. It was a mean and cruel thing to say, but slapping someone in real life is not like slapping someone in the movies. There is no victory or empowerment or dramatic romantic tension in it. A slap in real life just leaves your fingers burning and the lingering truth that something is irreversibly wrong. I ran into the house. I opened the door to my studio and collapsed onto the floor, sobbing. Brandon followed me.

"I'm sorry too," he looked down at me as I curled in a ball on the wood floor gasping for air. "But, you know, it's true . . . You're not okay. You're not well. It's like all the women in your family, your mom, your grandma, you all have the same thing, you're all sick. You need help." The sting of his assessment lingered like a paper cut. The women of my family? Sick?

My mother had been in and out of rehab since I was child. She was sober now, and dedicated to tribal social work, specifically child welfare. As an adult, her recovery affected me less, but I still struggled. Two years ago we had gone to the mall. We shopped and ate Thai food. Then, out in the car I clicked my seat belt closed, but my mom didn't start up the car. She pulled out a letter instead. I was used to her making amends; she had been doing it most of my childhood. I was accustomed to the apologies and the epiphanies, the *I'm sorry*s and *I love you*s. But that afternoon I just wanted my mom and me to be like the other moms and daughters walking together in the mall. I had come home and spilled my frustration all over the dining room table as Brandon and I tried to eat dinner. He was used to hearing about it. He knew my mom had also been assaulted as a child. He knew she began to drink as a teenager. He knew she had taken pills in secret and gone to rehab for it. He knew she and my grandmother were estranged. He also knew about my great-grandmother, my namesake, how she once stood against the waves of a roaring ocean, dark and suicidal. But to hear him say it made my face flush and my blood hot.

I closed my eyes to the sea of red. This time I sat blazing in it. I began to cry so loud the crying was more like yelling. And I pleaded for him to either get out or take me to the hospital.

Maybe I had lost my mind. Maybe I needed to be committed. I cried, curled in a circle on my floor, afraid. I was losing myself, slipping into some dark place. The fainting proved that. I'd crawl out and it yanked me back. Was I traveling into the spirit world? Was I completely coming unhinged? I quieted myself, I let myself breathe. He knew I wanted him to leave, that I wanted to rest alone. I heard the door shut behind me. I remained still, curled there, on the floor. Dreamlike, lyrics came into my head though there was no music. Words that stood stark against the small noise of my labored breath:

*You said of my family we were cursed, specifically
    the women . . . sick.*

Cutting the Blanket

After the big fight, I did not leave my room for a long time. I lay on the small bed in my writing studio, listening to Joy Division. "She's Lost Control" floated around the piles of books, homework, and records. Ian Curtis was singing about a woman with epilepsy, but I couldn't help seeing myself in those lyrics. I was losing control. My spirit was so sick that I was fainting, and my fainting was changing me. We knew without speaking it out loud that I was leaving. I had to. But still this nagging voice inside me begged me to reconsider. I looked around at the band posters, the paintings, the framed photos—this was my home. This was my linoleum.

My great-grandmother watched her mother's house go up in flames from a lawn chair. Her father built the house in the 1930s for her mother. It was a gift of love, made by his own hands, for his beloved. Finally, her mother had a place to lay her linoleum permanently. The house remained in the family for generations. I grew up spending time there. My cousins and I played there as children. A cozy, white cottage with two bedrooms, it had that kind of smell that made you feel like you were at home, old and familiar. My great-grandmother was in her eighties when the house caught fire, the damage too severe to repair.

"We have to burn it," she said. Medicine workers arrived early in the day, wearing white dresses and red paint. First they worked on my great-grandmother. Then they went to work on the house. After a prayer, the young men that accompanied them lit the four corners of the house. Then they watched it burn. When the fire marshal arrived, my uncle informed him that this was a ritual burning, spirit work. With a nod, the fire marshal left them to it, as an entire house went up in flames.

Our house didn't burn when Brandon and I left it. It sat empty, nothing but a sofa we couldn't get rid of and some hooks and wire still dotting the walls. All of our stuff went into a storage unit. He was going to stay at his parents' house. I planned to couch surf until I found something more permanent. I packed my car with the essentials, a couple bags of clothes, all the books I needed for grad school, and my laptop, but the packed car surfaced memories of the Swinomish church attic, the Thousand Trails campground, the bowling alley I had once slept in. I thought of the pallet of wood in the unfinished Petco. Not ready to leave yet, I told Brandon I'd stay one more night. There was a sofa, a box of leftover pizza, and a couple of beers. We shared the pizza and sipped the beer. We hadn't packed our wedding blanket, which I laid out on the sofa. Then I curled against him sad and quiet. I cried loud and long and hard. Brandon and I embraced before saying goodbye and he left reluctantly. He was still angry at me. He was hurt that I was giving up.

When a Coast Salish marriage ends, it is called "cutting the blanket." When two people no longer wish to be bonded beneath the same blanket, they cut the bond and release each other. In cutting our blanket, we left behind the ruins of a home.

Homelessness is a shaky feeling. Like a leaf clinging to a branch in the winter, trembling before it falls. That night I lay wrapped in my wedding blanket alone on the couch in the dark. The living room was big and empty without all of our stuff. It creaked and whined as if angry and abandoned. Big picture windows let in the streetlight. Cars rolled by in the endless rain. I thought of my great-grandmother watching her parents' house burn. The house had been struck by lightning. That's how the fire had started.

In our burning ceremonies we place the belongings of

our loved ones in a ritual fire. The smoke carries their possessions to the spirit world so they can have some of their comforts. The ritual also provides a way for us to let go, a way to ensure a spirit won't cling to us. It's a dangerous thing to cling to lost loved ones. It's important to release them. The lightning struck and my great-grandmother knew she needed to burn the rest of the house. She knew her mother was calling to it, to bring it back to her, her permanent home.

That night I tossed and turned uncomfortably on the small sofa beneath my wedding blanket. I looked around the room, unable to find whatever it was I needed to burn.

The Place of the Bracken Root

The good thing about my homelessness at thirty-three versus in my teens was that I was not surrounded by wayward children and drug addicts. I had a social network of friends with jobs and homes and stability. Those friends put me up and let me crash on their couches and their beds, and one let me rent a room month to month while I figured out my next step. Cricket and I met at a mutual friend's party. We bonded over shared stories of a wild childhood. She was blown away that I was couch surfing while simultaneously working on my graduate thesis.

Cricket's house was virtually empty apart from a mid-century modern coffee table standing stark against the empty room and white walls.

"Did you just move in?' I asked my first night in the house.

"Oh no," she laughed apologetically, "I've been here for months. I just got back from traveling and haven't set up. Kinda just moved back on a whim and don't really have that whole home thing down."

I looked down at the coffee table and smiled. "Well, you have that. That's a start." It was her linoleum.

Before Cricket and I met, I slept in my friend Ashley's bed some nights. As an unofficial roommate in a communal house, I tried to stay out of the house while she was at work. I wandered the neighborhood feeling like that transient teen I once was. At least I was doing well at school. I hadn't quit that, despite everything. I'd spend afternoons working in a drafty coffee shop with no heat. Without a stable home, thoughts of moving drifted into my imagination. Nothing was keeping me in Seattle. I could go anywhere.

I still texted Richard every day. We had long phone calls. Occasionally, I'd drive up north to see him. One sunny weekend I made the long drive up to Skagit Valley to hike with him. We drove up Chuckanut Drive, a scenic route outside the town we both grew up in, the one we met and fell in love in. Even in summer the forest was lush and green. The path lined in decaying logs was blanketed in moss, and sunlight crept in through the dense trees in beams of muted light. I passed a wild huckleberry bush and touched its soft leaves with my fingertips. The trail we were hiking intersected with the Pacific Crest Trail. I thought about all the women who might have walked it before me. My ancestors. College students. Writers. People trying to find themselves.

Richard and I hiked to the top of the Oyster Dome to celebrate him not having brain cancer. He'd had a cyst a couple years earlier, and before it was diagnosed, well, he thought he might have brain cancer. He had attempted to hike the Oyster Dome back then but never finished. During that time he wrote me a letter.

"I never gave it to you. Obviously. I just put all the things I felt down on paper and tucked it away in a drawer. I needed you to know . . ." He paused and lifted himself over a fallen tree. "If anything would have happened, I needed you to know I loved you, even after all this time."

Hearing Richard say that he still cared for me filled me with a deep sense of relief. I felt less alone in his confession. I had always cared for him too. His love had lit a secret candle in a dark corner of my heart. Like a tenant you just can't evict, that secret space had always been his.

We reached the top of the Oyster Dome. I saw the Cascade Mountains and the Samish Bay below. The Skagit River was somewhere down there winding through the trees. A yellow sun blazed in a cloudless, sapphire sky. We shared a beer in celebration as we admired the small green-and-blue world below. A couple of other hikers came and went. Our silence was comfortable.

"Is Brandon okay?" Of course Richard asked about Brandon. He was like that, kind, considerate, selfless.

"Not really." I shrugged and looked at the salmon-berry bushes that climbed up around the narrow path, their berries pink and juicy. "But I'm working on it. He's working on it." It was true. Brandon and I had been spending time apart and checking in as the weeks went by. I loved him. But I was angry at him, and my anger was debilitating and all-consuming. In my heartache I justified giving up. I justified leaving.

I returned my gaze to Richard. He hadn't changed much since that first night at the Vasa Hall. His face was still soft and delicate, with eyes the color of the moss on the trail we had just hiked, light brown hair, and eyebrows hung in a constant state of worry. "We should probably get down to the water and make camp," I said, glancing at the sky. I wanted to make it before dark.

We made it to Teddy Bear Cove just before sunset. Hippies had landscaped the small cove back in the sixties, and for many years it was a secret nude beach. Now it was just a cool place where locals came and camped. It had been one of our favorite places, and a deep peace found me as we scurried over the train tracks and stepped down onto the beach. We had the place to ourselves.

We set up camp and laid a blanket out next to the

water. I sipped whiskey. Richard drank beer and we played a game of cards. It was easy being close to him. I wondered what a life with Richard might look like. I pictured a small house not far from here, in Skagit Valley, where I had ties to the land and the river. He would make art. I would write. Richard would never lie to me, I thought. Richard didn't seem capable of deception. He would never take the first money we'd receive as a couple and secretly purchase a ticket to Australia with it. He would never abandon me. I let myself drift in and out of this fantasy as the night went on. As the sun set, the sky went from shades of gold to amber to indigo. The waves lapped at the stony shore and soon we were enveloped in night. Inside the tent he and I slipped into REI sleeping bags and listened to the ocean. My head scooted closer to his shoulder and I rested it there. I knew this was wrong, but I didn't care. I wanted to feel close to him, to feel loved, and to love him in return.

"Remember, I'm Robert Mapplethorpe and you're Patti Smith." We had both recently read Patti Smith's memoir *Just Kids* and had set a boundary for ourselves based on the deep love between the famous singer-songwriter and her beloved friend and muse, photographer Robert Mapplethorpe. Richard softly but sternly reminded me of our agreement: nothing would happen between us, not while I was still involved with Brandon, and not while I was still conflicted and shaken. But I was not

Patti Smith and Richard was not Robert Mapplethorpe. He was not and would never be just a friend. I fell asleep that night tortured by the desire I felt, the things I knew I could be capable of if he would let me. What was wrong with me? The question looped over and over in my head as I listened to the waves push the rocks up and down the shore. What was wrong with me? Brandon's words cut like a knife through that tent and into my sleeping bag and right into me: "The women in your family are sick . . ." Were we? Would I ever be better?

The sun woke me as the green walls of my tent began to sweat with condensation. I pulled the zipper up and crawled out onto the bright beach. For a moment I watched the tide ebb. Deep-green clumps of rubbery sea kelp littered the gray pebbles. Then I heard Richard's side of the tent unzip. He pulled a black wool hat over his head, rubbed his eyes, and joined me on the piece of driftwood where I sat.

I rested my head on his shoulder. "It's so beautiful here."

"It is."

"Can we live here?" I smiled.

"Yeah," he joked. "We can."

But we couldn't live there, so we broke down the tent and began to pack up our things.

We were quiet as we drove through the deep woods along the Samish Bay. At the Horseshoe Café, we shared hash browns and bad coffee and laughed about smelling like firewood and seaweed. I took my Instax camera out and snapped a photo of him. He looked sweet and sad, backlit in the morning sunlight. Then I flipped the bulky instant camera around at myself.

"I love you," I told Richard. "I have always loved you." But I stopped before really diving into my conflicted heart. I didn't want to cry in a booth at a crummy diner.

Richard looked at me across the table. "I know. I love you too. And who knows, maybe we find our way back to one another, through all of this. When it's right, you know? After all that's happened . . . maybe . . ." His voice trailed off, but it sounded hopeful.

We were in the college town of Bellingham in northern Washington, close to the Nooksack River. I also come from the Nooksack people. I literally had roots here. Our name, Nooksack, translates to "place of the bracken root," a dietary staple of the Nooksack people. As I poked at the remains of my breakfast, I looked around the Horseshoe Café and thought of the long drive back to Cricket's house in Seattle, one hour and thirty-five minutes on the interstate, and how badly I wanted to be home. Wherever home was now.

The Cranberry Marshes

Comptia Koholowish watched as her husband and his carpenters labored. Sawing, nailing, and digging the foundation of the new house. The European-style house was different from the large plank houses of her people, which were big enough to house several families. The captain's house was also big, but it was intended only for him. She could not get used to her new name, her English name. "Jane," her new husband would call to her, and it would take her several times to turn her head. She did not forget the sounds of Chinook words and songs. She remembered the feasts and the dances. With most of her tribe now gone, it had been many years since a proper salmon ceremony had taken place, but she still remembered how to prepare the first salmon of the season, though now she prepared it for the captain. She knew to remove the heart first and to cook it splayed and staked over an open fire, "Indian style," her husband called it. It was the way he preferred it.

She still knew how to weave cedar dresses and mats and how to tan hide, but now her clothing mimicked the clothing of the white settlers. Beneath her linen dresses and the wool blanket draped over her shoulders, Comptia still dotted her arms in blackberry juice and decorated her limbs in charcoal and water, using a needle to press it into the skin of her arms and legs. This is how the women she grew up with adorned themselves, and Comptia remembered them as she sank the needle into her skin again and again.

One afternoon Comptia accompanied her husband to court. The Scottish sea captain was charged with selling liquor to an Indian. Comptia knew her husband was guilty of this, had seen him do it. She had seen the men from her once great tribe, which dwindled now to numbers below a hundred, stagger away from the captain's house with jars gleaming golden in the moonlight. It was against the law for any native person to consume spirits, and any Indian who did manage to obtain liquor faced a severe penalty. But a larger case took precedence that day, and the captain's time before the court was brief, rushed. A man had been murdered in the Cranberry Marshes. Comptia knew the place well, remembered gathering berries there as a child. She could close her eyes to see the stretching marshlands decorated with the dark red beads of hundreds of berries.

Dozens of buildings had gone up around the area—some were used for trading, others for serving liquor. An Indian man had tried to enter one of the buildings along the marshes. This building was for serving food, and upon trying to enter, the man was bludgeoned with a paddle and killed instantly. The owner of the establishment, a white settler, was before the court with his case. The Indian man had been drunk, the settler argued. He had been acting in self-defense. The court agreed and dismissed the case.

Comptia walked with her husband back to the house. He had received a fine and been sent on his way. Comptia knew the great stores of whiskey and other spirits the captain had hiding away in his secret places. They arrived back to their land just before nightfall and Comptia looked up at the house. A pointed rooftop, a large porch, and leaded windows, the house was nearly complete. She would never live inside the house.

Blue

My temporary home in Seattle was starting to feel familiar. I found an air mattress for the floor, a Nick Cave poster for the wall, and some candles. It felt more like a clubhouse than a home, but still this was my hideout. White Christmas lights and candles illuminated my evenings spent reading or working on essays. I made an altar out of an old wooden stool and put my grandmother's picture on it with a can of salmon, a white candle, and some fresh cedar. The bare walls and the lack of true foundation made me remember the trailer. The years of being wayward and lost, unsure and unstable, continued haunting me.

When I was asked to read some poems at a local literary event, it seemed appropriate to read the one I called

"Blue." It was a poem about a lot of things, but it was rooted in the trailer, in the years just before I became transient. When I was thirteen years old I attempted to dye my hair blue with a packet of raspberry Kool-Aid. In my cramped room of our single-wide trailer I had pored over pop music and beautiful teenagers in fashion magazines. As owls hooted from the darkness of the trees just beyond my window, I craved what the photos promised me: pretty, punk, white people. Not mixed heritage, not Indian, or on a reservation. With heavy-lidded eyes, they slunk and hung in trash-decorated alleyways in leather jackets and mesh shirts. If they were poor it was on purpose and they made it look glamorous. I desperately wanted to leave the reservation, to never live in a church attic or a trailer again. Blue hair would transport me, I was sure of it. So I dyed my hair with a packet of Kool-Aid and it did nothing but run down my scalp and my face and stain my skin blue. My hair was too dark. My hair was not blond.

My Blue poem was also about Richard, the first time we kissed and our teenage exploration of our bodies. It was about how my sadness lived in my body and about my great-grandmother. It was about my Skagit name, taqʷšəblu, and how even in my name, the sound, the word, "blue" featured prominently.

I called Richard to tell him about the reading.

"The Blue poem?" Richard knew it.

"The Blue poem," I smiled. Before hanging up Richard apologized for living so far away and said he wished he could make it. I never expected him to drive down, but it was still nice to hear. I hadn't done many readings around the city, so this one felt like a big deal and I was nervous.

My closest friends rallied to be by my side. We had dinner at a small restaurant neighboring the venue. The evening lit a spark in me. I was almost done with my MFA program. Soon I would have a degree.

"You look like a writer today," my friend's dad said. He beamed at me over his glass of white wine. "You do, you look like a real poet tonight." We all laughed. But secretly his comment stirred up a small confidence in me. I didn't feel like a writer. And as far as my outfit, well, it wasn't out of the ordinary. I wore a small black dress and a pair of Doc Martens boots. I wore a wide-brim hat over my dark hair and a fire-engine-red lipstick. I didn't feel like a writer. I certainly didn't think I looked like one.

Inside the venue I trembled with nerves. I buzzed around the room feigning calm and collectedness. I felt like I was having miniature heart attacks every five minutes. Then Richard came walking up the sidewalk. I spotted him through the large window of the building. Immediately, my heart calmed. He came. He came all the way from the valley just to see me read. I felt like I did when we were kids, like he was holding my hand through a dark hallway or walking me through my first crowded punk show.

"You came!" I smiled and blushed.

"I did." He smiled back at me. We talked briefly and for a moment I was at peace. For a moment. Then, while he was walking across the small space to say hello to another friend, Brandon walked through the door. My heart sped up and almost stopped. He looked handsome, like Agent Cooper. My tall, dark, handsome, and somewhat estranged husband. *Shit*, I thought and walked directly over to him. He hugged me. I hugged him back, squeezing tightly.

"I thought your band had a show tonight." I was used to Brandon missing things.

His band booked a lot of shows.

"Oh, we do." His deep brown eyes met mine. His tone was soft, and he smiled. "But this is important to you. I wanted to surprise you." My heart fluttered, then tanked with guilt. Then practically fell out of my chest and onto the floor. Being in love with two people is like being drawn and quartered. I felt pulled apart. I felt torn. It was not fair to read the Blue poem in front of Brandon. I considered changing it, but how could I?

When they called my name to read, I looked at both Brandon and Richard. They couldn't be farther from each other in the small space and had only acknowledged

each other with a small nod. I made my way through
the crowded space to the microphone, then proceeded to
read a poem about being blue.

Shortly after I read, Brandon left to join his band.
And after a drink with Richard I said goodnight and
caught a lift back to Georgetown. I cried the whole car
ride home.

Later that night I was wide awake at three in the
morning. The nightmare wasn't unlike all the others that had plagued me throughout the year. I looked
around, realizing I was safe in bed. Moonlight came
in through the small window, casting the shadows of
a rhododendron tree across the carpet. I tried to slow
my breathing. I puffed my inhaler and took three vials
of kava tincture. I had to sleep, needed to sleep. I was
still waiting tables and had to open the restaurant in
the morning. I had some writing assignments due after that. The shadows of the leaves shook on the carpet
and I saw my bare room, my clubhouse, my temporary
space lit up in a panel of pale light. Seeing my shoes, my
piles of clothes, and my toiletries filled me with dread
again and I tried to blink the tears from my eyes. I tried
to blink the room and the moonlight and the bag out
of existence. Maybe if I closed my eyes long enough I
would open them in my own bed, in a room, in a house
that was mine.

On my laptop I saw the credits to *The Lost Boys* scrolling by. I must have drifted off right after that iconic boardwalk scene. I restarted it. Afraid to be alone, I put the earbuds in again and tried hard to fall asleep to my favorite eighties vampire movie.

Rose Quartz

Trying to distract yourself through immense heartache is like being at a party and trying to ignore the fact that your hair has caught fire. Still, I tried. I busied myself with graduate work. I went to shows, to parties, took unnecessary trips out of the city. I stayed out late, stayed gone long, everywhere I went the fire that crowned me followed, leaving behind its cloud of black smoke. I was a mess.

I visited a friend in Brooklyn. She took me out to fancy theater shows, art galleries, and rooftop parties. We spent the day at Coney Island. We rode the Wonder Wheel and tried to find the photo booth that Patti Smith and Robert Mapplethorpe loved. When we found the tarot reader, it was meant to be light. The fortune-teller looked me over as she pulled my cards, then before finishing the reading said plainly, "Your heart is broken." I looked up at her in the small tent we sat in and raised my eyebrows. I hadn't said anything. This stranger had pulled three cards, looked at me, and that was it. "Here," she placed a small stone in the palm of my hand, "you need this." I looked at the pale pink crystal. "It's rose quartz," she said sternly. "It's for the heart, and you need to surround yourself in it right now." I flew back to the West Coast a couple of days later, rolling the stone around in my fingers as we took off.

Back home I tried to stay put. I worked my shifts at the restaurant, worked on homework in local coffee shops. I went out with friends on the weekend. In the middle of a rowdy show at a punk venue, Brandon and I got smashed into the same corner of the crowd. We smiled delicately at each other, cautious. Then we ordered a drink at the bar. It turns out when you've shared ten years of your life with someone, it's not exactly easy to sever that tie.

We had been having dinner once a week at Cricket's. Living out of a space that wasn't fully mine had sparked an uneasy feeling inside me. Sleeping on a mattress on the floor of an empty room had brought me back to a time where I had no roots, no footing. Brandon's presence in the house grounded me. The time apart seemed to be good for us, and time together in small doses seemed manageable. Breakups are messy. Ours was no exception.

One night I stood before him in the orange streetlight that came in through my bedroom window. Something melted away as I let my dress fall to the floor. I no longer shook like a leaf at the thought of intimacy with him. I felt strong standing naked before him, and I wondered if I was ready to let him back in. We had slept together a lot. Each time it happened we wondered if it was the last time, but it never was. Still, my thoughts often turned to Richard. He was so dug into my heart that he was always a third presence in the room. I continued to entertain ideas of a home, a life with him in Skagit Valley. Blanket-wrapping ceremonies are strong things though. I couldn't deny that I remained tethered to Brandon. My heart still grieved over the cutting of our blanket.

Brandon traveled to Sweden for a music festival. While he was away, I visited Richard. We saw a show, walked along the river with my dog, and then went to a bar. After seeing the fortune-teller on Coney Island, rose quartz began showing up in my life. A gift from a friend or a necklace I happened to like in a shop turned out to be rose quartz. Soon I started to intentionally seek it out. I didn't want to be heartbroken anymore. I wanted to be well. A friend had brought me a huge rose quartz pendant from a flea market in Europe. I took to wearing it every day. The crystal was housed in an ornate casing that hung from a long metal chain. I loved the necklace—it was big and intense, old and strange, like something you might see on one of Dracula's concubines. I wore it everywhere, the crystal dangling just below my heart. That night at the bar Richard and I leaned close talking. I told him about seeing Brandon, how we had been slowly rekindling something. I told him I was confused. This didn't mean I didn't love him, too, only that maybe Brandon and I were going to work. Even as I spoke the words, the nagging voice in my head persisted: *But what about a life with Richard? What about a home? A real home.*

Then a friend recognized us and came to say hello. He knew the boys that I used to hang out with as a teenager. The boys who skateboarded. He brought this up like it was casual, and to him it probably was. But when he said, "Yeah, you used to date one of them right?" I felt weak and dizzy. One of them had been the one who assaulted me in the woods when I was sixteen, the one I couldn't get out of my head. I felt the rough rock against my cheek all over again. I smelled the sap on the breeze, heard the creek and the birds in the distance, and I lost it. I left the bar in a hurry, worried I might faint in the middle of the room, in front of everybody, in front of all of these terrible people from my childhood. I rushed out the door and onto the street. I started running. Tears fell down my cheeks as Richard followed close behind, worried and calling my name. Then I heard something shatter. I stopped and looked down at the pavement where my pendant lay in pink pieces at my feet. "No," I whispered, clutching a chunk of broken quartz to my chest. Something was wrong, wrong like a bad omen, wrong like a curse. I looked around half expecting to see the fortune-teller from Coney Island in the shadows, or something worse, waiting for me out there in the dark. All I saw was Richard, who calmed me, hugged me, and told me everything was okay. Still, I was worried. As I drove back to Seattle, I couldn't get the vision of the shattered crystal out of my head.

I emailed my old Intro to Jewelry and Metals instructor and asked him how to mend the crystal. But even epoxied back together, the crystal was still broken, the cracked lines where it shattered clearly visible. I hated looking at it this way, so I tucked it away in a drawer and forgot about it.

I busied myself with writing and working. I missed Brandon. Then I came down with a flu. A bad stomach bug. The bug persisted. I woke up sweaty and sick. Then it occurred to me: I hadn't needed a tampon in a while.

Peeing on a plastic stick was not something intuitive for me. How do you not splash your fingers in urine? Annoyed and anxious, I set the little plastic wand on the bathroom countertop and waited. Three minutes felt like three hours. When I finally yanked the test up and read the results, I saw two little lines. Twin dashes bled into the cotton, pale pink and identical. I looked at the symbol cradled in my fingertips. Faint and dizzy, all I could think about was the color: rose quartz.

Heaven Tonight

Brandon needed to know I was pregnant, but he was still in Sweden. We were not technically back together, and I worried that the news that he'd gotten me pregnant might not be the easiest thing for him to receive at such a distance. I was afraid of what our friends might think if I told them. Kids were not a common thing in our friend group. We were musicians, artists, painters, writers, and in some cases just complete fuckups. Kids didn't really happen too often in my social circle.

I needed to tell someone I trusted, someone who loved me unconditionally, someone who wouldn't judge me. So I got in my car and drove straight to Richard's house. When I arrived, Richard was working on one of his art pieces. He let me in and turned down the music, and we both sat on the sofa. I pulled out the pink-and-lavender cardboard box. I had purchased another test on my way up. Perhaps the first one had been wrong.

"I can't do this alone," I told him. His face contorted into a frown. He was quiet. "I'm sorry," I tried to explain, "I just really need someone. If it's . . . positive." I went into the bathroom. I tried to brace myself, to be strong. I peed on the little stick again and waited. I swung the bathroom door open and sat on the edge of the tub. Richard joined me. When I flipped it over, the same rose quartz lines greeted me. I dropped the wand to the ground. "Oh my fucking god," I said. Then I held my belly. Something was inside there. Something was growing inside my body. This immediately made me think of the movie *Alien*. I thought of facehuggers and things bursting out of me, bloody and violent. Terror swept over me. I was shaking, my breath sputtering, and I dug my inhaler out of my bag and took a puff. A sweet, sickening feeling overcame me. Was it joy? Was it joy and terror at the same time? I looked at Richard, who seemed to have shattered in under a minute. He sat next to me crying into his hands. I froze. "Whoa," I put a hand on his back to try and stop the trembling. "Hey, this doesn't mean I'm getting back together with Brandon." I wasn't even sure if what I was saying was true; I wasn't sure of anything in that moment. "But I want this." Then my voice started to crack, then my own tears came. "I *want* this." I was holding my belly.

"I *want* to be a *mom*." Richard said nothing but continued to cry quietly next to me. "Look, Brandon and I will be in each other's lives, obviously, now, I guess, well, forever. But that doesn't mean that's where I end up." I tried to sound convincing. I tried to comfort my friend, my love, but the truth was I wasn't sure of anything anymore. Nothing was certain, except for those two pink lines staring back at me. Those were the only absolute. Then my anxiety rose up, big and overwhelming, huge inside my chest. I felt the bathroom walls start to close in on me.

"I need some air," I blurted. If my tone seemed harsh, I hadn't meant for it to, but I was vibrating with adrenaline. I rushed out of the candlelit bathroom and through the living room where I had spent so many evenings with Richard. The gas fireplace flickered orange and amber, casting light and shadows along the walls where dozens of oil paintings hung in their ornate golden frames. I loved this room. I blinked tears out of my eyes, remembering us reading poems on the floor, looking at art books, and talking about our childhood, but I couldn't stay there. I left the cozy living room and stepped into the cold night.

I ran. The walls of the house had been crushing me, shrinking. Now the vast blackness of the night sky and all the twinkling stars seemed to do the same. I passed the houses, the parked cars, and the streetlights. I kept going, like I could somehow outrun my fear, those pink lines, my brokenhearted friend, my angry husband. I passed the

Vasa Hall, the site of the first punk show I ever went to, the parking lot where I met Richard. I reached the fair-grounds. I kept going until I was in the center of the large open lawn and collapsed. Under the stars, in the cold night, I sat alone in the dark and cried. I wasn't sure what time it was in Yellowknife, but I pulled out my phone and dialed Tania's number. Tania was my best friend at the Institute of American Indian Arts and she was the strongest woman I knew. I don't think I had ever been more thankful to hear the words "Hey girl . . ." through my phone than I was that night. She was awake, busy with her beadwork. Her voice poured through the phone warm and sweet and lit up the dark around me like an oil lamp. I felt myself smile.

"I'm pregnant, Tania. I'm fucking pregnant." Though she was miles and miles north of me, someplace near the Arctic Circle, I felt her with me as we talked.

"Why are you alone?" she asked in her blunt accent, something I loved about her. Tania was G'wichin and Swedish and raised in France. She had a strangely beautiful accent. "Where is Brandon?"

"Sweden."

"Where is Richard?"

"Back at the house, upset."

"Oh my god." The words punched through the phone, knifelike.

She was disappointed. She told me that. Then she

told me, "You don't need them, Sasha." When she said my name it came out overenunciated—*SA-shaaa*—a quirk of her accent that always made me smile. "And you know what? You want this. And you're going to be okay." I realized something as she spoke. All I'd needed was that, to hear that I was going to be okay. It was that easy.

I drove back to Seattle, barreling down the freeway at eighty miles per hour while my thoughts raced. I had so much to do. I had to find a place to live. A permanent place. I had to go to the doctor. I had to tell Brandon. The climbing wall of fir trees and cedars gave way to houses, then apartment complexes, then shopping centers, then the tall buildings of downtown. I drove along the water and then through the industrial district. I saw the port and the cranes and finally reached my neighborhood. When I pulled up to Cricket's house, I thought about my mattress on the floor, the string of café lights and vintage frames I had hung for ambience, and the antique end table with a lace doily on top I used as a nightstand. All of my things were still in storage, and given what I had to work with, some hand-me-downs and some treasures from a nearby Goodwill, I had made the little room inhabitable. But it was temporary. I touched my belly as I walked up the house's front steps. I couldn't afford to be temporary anymore.

Brandon came home five days later, and I offered to pick him up from the airport. I wasn't subtle. He threw his bags in the back of my car and hopped in the passenger seat. I pulled the white plastic wand out of my cup holder and handed it to him with the two pink dashes in the result window facing up. "Hi," I said.

"Oh!" he replied. Before I started the car, I took a deep breath.

"I don't know what this means for us. I know I still want to be on my own. I know I want to live on my own. But I want this baby. I really, really want this baby."

"So do I." He took my hand and we pulled each other into a hug. On the drive home we talked about a lot of things. Mostly about me needing to find a place to live more permanently.

"This isn't going to fix anything," I said. "But I know we care for each other. I know we love each other. We can do this together. But this isn't a Band-Aid. We're not pregnant and all of a sudden I trust you again or whatever, right?" Brandon rolled his eyes but nodded his head in agreement. We drove the rest of the way back to Cricket's house in a mix of anticipation, anxiety, and a familiar comfort.

In the weeks that followed I adamantly searched for a more suitable housing situation. I went to my doctor's appointments at the Seattle Indian Health Board. I didn't tell anyone else about my pregnancy. I wasn't sure how yet. Instead I kept going to shows, enjoying soda water with lime, and getting tired before the last band began.

I'd show up to art shows and parties, politely declining wine when it was offered. "I'm on a cleanse" was my excuse. And my friends would smile without question. I even saved up two nights' worth of tips to buy a Vitamix. I realized I was good at being pregnant.

Then I realized I was happy. One sunny morning I walked through the neighborhood on my way to work. I stepped over fallen petals from the trees, and though it was a cold day, the sun was shining on the wet Seattle pavement. With my earbuds in I hummed along with Courtney Love. I was listening to Hole's poppy album, *Celebrity Skin*, the record no one wanted to admit liking. I was listening to the song "Heaven Tonight." Courtney Love wrote the song in order to have something to sing to her daughter, Frances Bean Cobain. She wanted to have something to sing to her at night. The song had always been a guilty pleasure, its overly saccharine melody and Love's raspy voice, her scratchy vocals over the tune like gravel on honey. I hated that I liked Hole, but I did. I hated that I liked this album, but I did. First I hummed, smiling as I walked alone, then with my hand on my belly I just straight-up started singing. When Courtney Love's cat-scratching voice sang the refrain, I couldn't help but smile a little. Humming along I had to laugh at the absurdity of it. I was still a waitress at a pizza place. I still had not found my footing through the divorce, or finished my MFA, or had one single sliver of direction, but I knew this. I knew I was going to have this baby, and I dreamt she'd be a girl.

In an interview, Love had denied that the song was about her daughter and said that instead it was about a girl driving down the Pacific Coast Highway on her way to see her boyfriend. The girl in the song, according to Love, was on her way to lose her virginity to her boyfriend, thus going to "heaven tonight," but instead she's blindsided by a truck and killed. I didn't let this bit of musical trivia ruin my mood as it crept into my thoughts. I just kept walking, noticing each fallen petal on the pavement as I stepped over it, pink and delicate.

The Carver

They gave me my first ultrasound at eight weeks. It was early, but the doctors wanted to be sure nothing was abnormal. I had a history of cysts and fibroids, and the doctors were sure I had endometriosis. When my hormone levels weren't rising at the rate of a typical pregnancy, they called me in for the ultrasound. They printed out a little picture pointing out the gestational sac and told me, "There's your baby, right where it's supposed to be." It wasn't in one of the fallopian tubes like they might have suspected.

"It looks like the Death Star," Brandon laughed when I showed it to him later that day.

"Don't say our baby looks like the Death Star!" I laughed too and snatched the photo from him, placing it next to four blue candles on my altar. Blue was for protection.

After Brandon left, I lit a bundle of cedar and filled my room with its sweet smoke. The sun came in through my window while I thumbed through a book on pregnancy that Tania had gifted me. It had come in a package along with an old photograph of a beautiful native mother holding her baby. She also included an old David Bowie T-shirt I'd left at her house and a pair of dentalium earrings that she made. Dentalium was traded between our two tribes. The delicate, narrow shells were white, and she had strung antique red beads along the ends of them. The earrings hung down to my shoulders, long and elegant.

"Dentalium was a symbol of wealth," the card read. "We wear it to show how much we are loved." I hadn't taken the earrings off since the package arrived.

I set the book down on the carpet and looked at a hobbit jade I kept on my windowsill. The jade was a Christmas gift from a friend. I had followed her instructions, potted and watered the thing accordingly. I frowned at its wilted edges. How was I supposed to take care of anything? I couldn't even take care of this plant, and jade plants were practically indestructible.

A figure passing by distracted me from my sad jade. He was in his midforties and dirty. In his hand he held a half-empty bottle of Steel Reserve. His face was creased with age, but beneath the grime I could see he was handsome. I didn't know what tribe the man was from, but I knew he was Coast Salish. He wore a bandanna across his forehead, low on his brow, and his thick black hair hung to his shoulders. The man stopped, adjusted his pants, and tanked the rest of the bottle before tossing it into the front yard. He retrieved another one from his orange JanSport backpack and kept walking, toward the Duwamish River, beyond the factories and the warehouses.

Seeing the man made me think of my uncle Ron. He was also handsome, stoic with long dark tresses and a broad Hollywood native face. Women loved him. Uncle Ron was an artist—a painter, a teacher, and a carver—and this fascinated me as a child. My uncle was a red paint dancer. He knew the traditional ways as well as the contemporary, having grown up close to his Salish culture while also studying painting at a fine-arts college in Seattle. He moved through both worlds. When he was young his grandmother took him into the longhouse, where he was instructed to be quiet, and well behaved, and to listen. Right away, my uncle knew the power of the winter ceremonies and would later enter the longhouse as a grown man to become a spirit dancer. Uncle Ron called my mom Jillybean and seemed to adore her. Though he was intimidating, he had something about him, something warm and protective. As a kid, I constantly tried to impress him. I'd draw him pictures and he'd tell me he was proud of me and I'd beam with pride. My uncle never married, not for good, and he never settled down into a family. Instead, he was committed to his art, creating beautiful pieces that still hang in galleries today, pieces that depict our Coast Salish way of life. It was as if he felt obligated to capture the culture and keep it from disappearing. Like my great-grandmother who worked to revive our traditional language, my uncle knew the danger, the extinction, we faced and did what he could to stop it.

My uncle talked about the longhouse. He talked about the smoke stinging your eyes, the cold dirt floor, the warmth of the fire and the smell of smoke deep in your clothes, but he never disrespected the privacy of the dances, and he never spoke about the details. This was out of respect as well as a need to protect the sacred. My Salish ancestors lost the right to practice their ceremonies in the early years of white settlement. When my uncle painted the longhouse scenes, he did so because he wanted to educate people. He wanted to share with the world what we had been forced to abandon for a brief time. Perhaps he was trying to heal that injustice. His paintings were considered taboo by some. But my uncle felt called by his spirit to do this, and when your spirit calls you to do something, you listen. He had learned that.

I knew the power these paintings held firsthand. Even as a small child, the paintings captivated me. Each brushstroke, each line, each face splashed in red told a story, one that felt loud and heavy, like drums. My uncle quietly struggled at different times in his life with alcohol, never letting it consume him fully. Perhaps it was the challenge of his work that troubled him, or perhaps it was the sadness he battled, the sadness of trying to balance being Indian in a white world. My grandmother used to tell me he was born in the wrong time. She'd smile. "He would have carved canoes, and made beautiful artwork. If he had been born in the old days he would have been happy. Handsome Indian man like that, but this world wasn't right for him. He was meant to live back then." Her voice grew shaky when she said the last part. We had lost him to diabetes. She'd shake her head and say, "He was born in the wrong time."

I stood at the window and closed my eyes. I tried to imagine the land when it was still forested, before the river was polluted, before the settlers and the factories. I wondered what the man outside my window did, before he wandered the streets with a backpack full of Steel Reserve. Maybe he would have been a carver. Maybe he, too, was born in the wrong time.

Tidelands

The weeks went by. I took my prenatal vitamins and continued to get blood work done at the Seattle Indian Health Board. They wanted to keep an eye on my hormone levels. I kept searching for a more suitable living situation but eventually became overwhelmed. I decided that a weekend in Portland would help, so I boarded the Amtrak on a gray afternoon, heading south. I wanted to visit friends, roam Powell's Books, and get away from Seattle. As the train sped down the tracks along the river, I restlessly watched the jade-green water move against the snow-covered boulders and cedar trees. I couldn't relax. My body shook with panic. I didn't just fidget or fuss, I quaked, like my body was some unknown planet, its core shifting and unstable. I paced the train's narrow walkways. Worry had moved into my body and it was infecting every cell. Where was I going to live? What was I going to do? My scholarship would run out soon. I would graduate. Was I going to be a writer? A mother? A wife? Was I going to be homeless? I sat down, then got up, then sat down again. In the dining car I sat at a table and ate a package of saltines. Then my phone alerted me to a new email.

Timing is a mysterious thing, and when I opened that email on the Amtrak I was in disbelief. I thought I read it wrong, so I reread it. I did this twice. A woman from the Lummi tribe had been trying to reach me for months regarding my land. *My land?* Surely the woman had been mistaken. What land? I called my mom.

"What is she talking about?" My mouth was dry from saltines and anxiety.

"Grandma had land in Lummi," my mother confirmed, then added, "Where are you headed now?" She had grown accustomed to my habit of running away.

"Portland," I said with a sigh. "I wanted to visit some friends."

"Well, come back soon. You might want to check into this."

As the train continued to bullet through the trees into Oregon, the worry transformed into wonder. Somewhere out there was a parcel of land with my name on it. Soon

I was mellow enough to fall asleep with my head against the glass.

I cut my trip to Portland short and was headed back north within two days. I drove past Skagit Valley, past Bellingham, to the Lummi tribal offices. The woman who had emailed me was short and round. She smiled when she shook my hand. She gave me the paperwork followed by directions and a map.

The property was located twenty minutes outside of the city, in Lummi Bay. To the west were the San Juan Islands, to the east was Mount Baker, and the Canadian border was just a few miles north. I walked the road for a bit; nothing but an old trailer and some appliances stood on the property. I stepped down into the grass. The ground was wet, and my boots sank into the mud. *Why is Indian land always like this?* I looked around. Apart from the very edge of the property where someone had scooted their trailer and some old television sets close to the highway, the land was uninhabitable. It was tideland. A small river curled through the grass and made its way out to the bay. I smiled. My great-grandma had given me a marsh. *Why?*

Walking back up to the road, I noticed how beautiful the surrounding area was, the mountains, the bay, the hills of tall trees. Then I looked back out to this land, to the land that over a hundred years ago was given to the Lummi tribe by the federal government. This was not prime land. Did the Lummi know that then? When they signed treaties, when they settled for whatever was left to them, did they know this land was unlivable?

Perhaps I could build a house out there. It would have to be on stilts, but I would be close to the Skagit River, to where my great-grandmother grew up. I would be close to Richard, but so far from Brandon and my life in Seattle. I sat down on the side of the road next to my parked car. The paperwork bore my great-grandmother's signature. I saw the place where it named me her heir, but why had she given this to me? I closed my eyes and saw her handwriting. A lump in my throat came on fast and my face flushed. I buried my face in my knees and cried on the side of the road next to a piece of land that had been passed down to her by a Lummi relative and now, for whatever reason, was mine. I thought of our name, taqʷšəblu. She had given me that as well. Then I heard her voice in my head: "You're my namesake, and you're going to do important things."

The Lummi tribe wanted to buy back the land. My nonnative friends advised me to hold on to it. "Real estate only increases in value, don't sell!" they said. This felt gross to me. The land was technically mine, but I didn't feel any connection to it or ownership over it. If the tribe wanted it back, shouldn't they have it back? My white friends shook their heads, confused by this. I sold the land back to the tribe, but before I signed the paperwork I went back once more. I walked along the mud, looked out to the water. I dug my fingernails into the swampy earth and whispered, "Thank you."

"Are you sure they gave you enough money for it?" some of my friends would ask, concerned that my lack of knowledge on land value might have gotten me duped. A knot would twist in my belly and I'd just smile and shrug, "Probably."

I hadn't told anyone else about the pregnancy. Just Cricket, Brandon, Richard, and Tania. I wanted to wait until it was impossible not to, or at least until after graduation. I hadn't even told my mother. Instead I busied myself with my work, went to PTSD therapy for survivors of sexual violence, and looked for a home. I spoke with Tania on the phone as much as I could.

One rainy afternoon, I was sitting cross-legged on my grandmother's sheepskin rug, one of the only things I had purposefully not tucked away in storage. I was reading about Comptia. For my thesis I was researching the women of my family. We had all gone through so much. This afternoon I was reading about how Comptia survived the smallpox epidemic. I closed my eyes and pictured young faces ruined by blisters and boils. Comptia had walked away from smallpox, but what had I done?

I didn't want to have PTSD anymore. I didn't want the memory of my assault to ruin me anymore.

My phone rang. It was my mother wanting to know if I wanted to come to Tacoma to look at the house my grandmother was selling. I hadn't thought of my dad's mother's house since the day I stopped breathing in the back of my parents' car. I closed my eyes and saw the house, blue with white trim, a yard with a cedar tree and a scattering of rose bushes. I ran the length of grass as a child, explored the basement, and laughed with cousins on the back porch as the sun set behind the hills. I thought of Comptia.

With the money from the sale of the land, I bought the house in Tacoma. Just like that, I wasn't homeless anymore. The night before I moved in, I dreamt of my uncle, the artist. In the dream he followed me around the large two-story house, quietly nodding and smiling as I went from room to room. A strange sensation overwhelmed me when I woke, like he had been there, in the room with me. I had never dreamt of him before.

As my mom helped me unload boxes into my new house, I told her about the dream. She set a box of books down and looked at me. "Well, that makes sense." She smiled, brushed a long hair from her face, and added, "Uncle Ron was very protective of us. He was just checking on you." She said it affectionately, before heading back out to the car. When she was safely out of sight, I patted my tummy.

"Hear that?" I smiled and spoke to my own body. "Uncle Ron was checking on us." I looked around the house. It was spacious and beautiful. Brandon had helped me with the painting and flooring. Together we made it something I could be happy in, somewhere I could raise our kid, and a place to write. My permanent home. The unpacked boxes, the lamp, the chair, these things were mine, my linoleum.

The Last Indian Princess

As I was settling into my new home, Brandon's family took us to Hawaii. The trip was brief, luxurious, and uncomfortable. "I wish you guys would just get back together," his mom would say with a sigh and an eye roll. I'd smile apologetically, unsure of what to say to the woman who had paid for a beautiful wedding for a failed marriage. Being with Brandon was beginning to feel like some semblance of home, though, and as I worked in the open dining room of the vacation rental on Kauai surrounded by the rich aroma of tropical plants, I began to wonder if we had a chance.

We did tourist things with his family, and as grateful as I was for such an extravagant gift, I hated being a tourist in a place so recently colonized. To see things like sugar plantations and missionary museums made my stomach uneasy. On our second-to-last day on the island I woke up spotting blood. Terrified, I woke Brandon, who rushed me immediately to the island's urgent care clinic. I sat nervously in the waiting room, wondering why all the doctors were white. When they gave me a pelvic exam, they found nothing wrong. My cervix was normal. This was not a miscarriage. "Spotting is normal," they said and suggested I follow up with my regular doctor before sending me on my way.

Back in Seattle my doctors gave me another ultrasound. My former sister-in-law held my hand as the screen came into view. "There's your baby," the technician smiled warmly and pointed to a plum-shaped thing on the screen. The Death Star had grown significantly in the past few weeks, and I smiled at the little kidney-bean-shaped person my body was making. "That's a normal, healthy heartbeat," she added. My sister-in-law and I went out for tacos and passion-fruit tea to celebrate.

I returned to Tacoma and unpacked the house, trying to set up as best I could the perfect home. When some of my nonnative friends, spoiled by Seattle, pulled up to my new home on the east side of Tacoma, they'd eye the boarded-up house next to me, take note of the lack of a Whole Foods or a coffee shop within walking distance. "Are you sure you're gonna be okay here?"

they'd ask. It's true, on the Indian allotment part of the city, we just had a couple of gas stations, a bar with no windows, a casino, and a smoke shop called the War Pony with a drive-through window.

"It's just poverty," I said. "I'm fine." In fact, I had never felt safer within the walls of a home. I had been coming here since childhood, and the house was filled with a generational energy. The weeks I spent sleeping alone in the house as I unpacked and settled in never spooked me. It was a difficult thing to explain to them, my friends who didn't grow up in that Indian way.

Still, inside they all softened. We had transformed the house into a beautiful sanctuary with new floors and a faux finish on the walls that made them look antique. I swelled with pride as I gave my friends the tour. My room was painted a soft gray and had a little balcony and a writing nook. The room was warm and light.

On the afternoon I walked Cricket through the house, I felt a particular relief. I was sure she was happy to have her space back. We passed the only unfinished room. "This is gonna be her room," I said, my eyes widening. We both laughed a little. It was still such a strange thing. I was having a baby.

The room was painted a warm gray.

"But what's the theme?" Cricket asked. The furthest I'd come was picking out a giant wall decal that made it look like an enchanted forest was right outside the room and a night-light in the shape of the moon. "Full-blown nerd?" she laughed.

"Full-blown nerd," I nodded. It was true. I was a giant nerd. And I wanted my daughter to love witches and wizards and magic. I wanted her to love fairy tales and myths. I wanted to build a space for her to escape into, where she could feel safe. When I lost myself in books as a kid, I was able to leave the sadness behind. I fell in love with magic, with spells, because of their power to change things. It was silly, to plaster a castle on the wall of my child's room, but I wanted her to have another world, something beyond the Indian allotment, the east side of Tacoma, beyond the reservation.

"The house is really beautiful." Cricket hugged me as I walked her to her car. "And you're right, it feels, I don't know, safe here. It feels good." I looked around. The sunlight was pouring over the large, fenced-in yard, flowers still bloomed, and jasmine crawled up the front porch. It's true we had no Whole Foods. But it wasn't like the reservation I grew up on, in the dark woods of rural Washington. This wasn't a single-wide trailer, buried in the cedar trees and close to predators. True, there was an abandoned house or two in my neighborhood, but the neighbors that were here were kind. The house sat on a hill, and from my window I could see the water, the Olympic Mountains, the shining buildings of downtown. It was a beautiful home.

—

It's funny how your body tries to tell you things, even if you try not to listen. After Cricket drove away that afternoon, my stomach felt queasy. I felt off. I had never been three months pregnant before, this was just part of it, I told myself. I kept telling myself I was okay. I went over the last ultrasound again and again. "There's the heartbeat," the woman had said. "I see a healthy, happy heartbeat, and next time, we'll know the sex." I already knew I was having a girl. My body had told me that too. I could feel her. I had dreamt of her.

Still, anxiety began to rise up in me and I paced back and forth. I thought of the emergency room on Kauai—"This is not a miscarriage. Everything is looking good."—trying to channel the doctor's words like a mantra. That night Brandon and I had plans for dinner. I was so distracted I hadn't even heard him knock.

"Jesus, what's wrong?" He came to my side, put his hand on the small of my back and my chest slowed. I couldn't calm down, not fully. I went to my altar, burned cedar, burned sage, lit candle after candle. He ran a bath for me, and as hard as I tried, I couldn't sit still long enough to be in it. I turned again and again, hugged my knees to my chest, sucked at the air.

"It's just a panic attack," he reassured me. "You've had them before."

He wasn't wrong. I knew the irrational motor of my heart as it took off without me. I knew my asthma, my PTSD, and my triggered responses. Still, my body was doing something I could not recognize. It was speaking to me in a foreign language, and I couldn't understand.

For an hour I kept going to pee. Even if I didn't have to, even if it was just to sit on the toilet and wipe, relieved every time there was no blood. *It's okay*, I'd tell myself, *see, no blood. It is okay. It's going to be okay.*

Brandon suggested we go to the movies, and I nodded. I knew I had to stop obsessing. We drove to the Southcenter mall and purchased two tickets to the only ten o'clock showing, some movie about a superhero.

I squirmed in my chair uncomfortably and tried to let Hugh Jackman's scowl and bad attitude distract me. There were car chases and fight scenes, a little girl, possibly a baby wolverine, and a lot of terrible dialogue.

Halfway through the movie I peed in my theater seat. At least I thought I did. I shot up and pushed through the cramped aisle of the theater. I ran to the bathroom, and when I sat on the toilet I was sure I had peed. I rose and found the bowl bright red. Dizzy, I made my way out to the hall. Brandon was waiting for me, worried. I fell down against him. He rushed me to the car, pulling me along, my feet barely moving. Somehow he got me across the vast expanse of the parking lot and to the car. As he walked around to unlock my side, I felt another gush. I put my hands between my legs and when I pulled them up to my face, they were shiny and red beneath the streetlight. I don't think I've ever made a sound like that, deep and guttural, not a growl, not a cry, not a scream, but like all of them combined. The most primal noise I had ever heard and it came from my own body. I was losing her.

Brandon sped to the emergency room. Lights blurred outside my window like neon streaks of rain. Everything felt far away and hazy. Inside the hospital they made us wait. And wait. And wait some more. When they did finally call us back for an ultrasound it only meant more waiting, only this time I was pants-less, with my feet in cold metal stirrups.

"Remember Hawaii?" Brandon held on to my hand. I remembered: I'd been given a pelvic exam. They hadn't had the equipment to do an ultrasound, but based on what they felt when they examined my cervix, they'd confirmed it wasn't anything to be alarmed about. "Remember, they said you're almost out of the woods. They said bleeding is normal." He was trying to be calm. He was trying to be strong for both of us. A tank of a Russian woman came in, ice cold. She put the wand inside me and said nothing. The screen in front of me that usually played back whatever was happening inside my womb, in a black-and-white abstract universe, remained blank.

"Why isn't the screen on?" My voice was shaking. "Can you turn it on? What's happening?"

"We only do that when the doctor is here." She prodded the wand more, her eyes glued to a screen only she could see.

"Please," I knew I sounded pathetic. And I knew she couldn't tell me anything, but I asked anyway. I asked again and again while tears ran down my cheeks. "Please tell me. Do you see her? Do you see her heartbeat? Do you see her? Can you just tell me if you see her?"

The woman pulled the wand from my body and stood up without saying anything. She reached the door before looking back. "They'll come for you." And the door fell closed behind her. Then there was nothing. Just the sound of my breath, of Brandon's breath. They came for me at two in the morning and wheeled me into a waiting room. I waited more.

"It's going to be just like Hawaii, isn't it?" I squeezed Brandon's hand. "Isn't it?" All he could do was squeeze my hand and nod back. We waited and waited. Eventually, a doctor came in carrying a clipboard that he didn't look up from. He cut through the waiting in six syllables.

"This is a miscarriage."

No sound came from my body. I just stared at the doctor, young, white, blond. I vibrated with anger as he droned on about my body passing the fetus within the next twenty-four hours. Something about pain meds. I didn't listen. I didn't hear anything but the faint buzzing of the fluorescent light above me. All I could see were the beige walls, Brandon's patient nod. I was quiet. I remained quiet as Brandon drove me to his parents' house, where he had been staying ever since we moved out of our shared home. Inside, my sister-in-law prepared me a sandwich and told me she loved me and that I'd need food at some point. His mother gave me a sedative and everyone went to bed. At five in the morning my body shot up in a panic.

"Brandon." I shook his arm. "Brandon . . . Brandon. Wake up. Something is wrong." He turned over on his side and mumbled. I shook again. Nothing. "Bran, please . . ."

"Yeah, the doctors said this would happen, remember?" Brandon said in one sleepy, breathy sentence, almost a whisper, and fell immediately back to sleep. I groaned and held my stomach. I tossed and turned violently. I continued to shake him. He continued to sleep. When I couldn't take it any longer, I struggled to my feet. I clung to the railing as I crept down the stairs. His parents' house was big, with tall ceilings and windows. Dawn seeped in through the windows casting a faint blue light. I inched past the fancy dining room, the chandelier, and into the spacious living room. Pain twisted my womb like a knife. I crumpled to the floor and cried out. I felt my body opening, the pains of it pulling apart. I writhed on a beautiful rug as the sun came up, giving birth, seven months early and alone.

At some point the pain released me, and I felt something else, something different.

Something was coming. I crawled to the bathtub.
Blood ran through me like a faucet until something else
made its way through my wrecked body, something I
caught and held in the palm of my hand. Half-naked and
trembling in a pool of deep, dark red, I held her.

I was afraid, but I slowly opened my fist. There she
was. In a plum-sized sack. Violet and red. I saw her little
body, curled like a pink petal, toes the size of seeds, small
eyelids, closed and blue.

Then I woke the whole house with a blood-curdling
scream. I didn't stop screaming. I couldn't. Brandon
picked me up and took her from me. He wrapped her in a
washcloth while I screamed. I screamed as he led me up
the stairs, all the way down the hall, and to the bedroom.
I screamed when he pulled the covers back and laid me
down. He put two white pills in my mouth, tipped a glass
of water to my lips, and quieted me. Then I slept.

———

My great-great-great-grandmother was named Myrtle
Johnson Woodcock. She was born on April 13, 1889, in
a small fishing village in the Washington Territory. The
settlers called her "The Last Indian Princess" because on
the day of her birth the ruling chiefs in the area traveled by
canoe to pay a ceremonial visit. They arrived in ornate canoes, bringing gifts and food. She was the granddaughter

of Chief Uhlahnee and the great-granddaughter of Chief Hoqueem. The settlers watched as the Quinault chief came ashore on the gray sand of the rocky beach in a forty-foot canoe, its high prow carved into a massive wolf's head. When she was born, the settlers knew my great-great-great-grandmother was important.

On the day of my daughter's birth, I buried her beneath a large cedar tree. There were no gifts or ceremonial visits. Just me and her father, beneath the bows of a cedar. I wanted canoes on the shore. She deserved feasts and songs. I wanted salmon and stories.

A lot of women have miscarriages; some have many. Women are accustomed to pain and grief. But as I stood beneath the tall cedar on the only birthday my daughter would ever have, I could not help but think of the Last Indian Princess. The same blood that brought the chief's canoes ashore over a hundred years ago also coursed through me, and now I had to bury it in the earth and leave my daughter there.

The Shed

When her husband's house was completed, Comptia
Koholowish moved into her own new dwelling. It was a
shed with four walls and a dirt floor on the edge of the
property line. It was a marriage of convenience for the
captain. Any white settler who married a native person
was given twice the allotment of land. As the captain built
his home on her land, Comptia was made to sleep outside. Indians weren't allowed in the house.

The first night Comptia slept in her new "home,"
she felt the cold draft of ocean air. Through her single
window she could look up at the captain's grand house.
As she sat in the lamplit dark eating her dinner alone,
she watched the captain move through the house. She

followed the glow of his oil lamp as it moved up the stairs and into the master bedroom.

She grew up sleeping in the plank houses of her people. She was accustomed to the drafts and the darkness. But in her childhood home she was fed and warmed by the fire. She was surrounded by family and songs and stories. In the shed she sat alone, secluded on her own ancestral land.

She fell asleep in the pitch-black darkness of her new home, remembering the light and laughter of her village, the abundance of fish and berries. She hoped in dreams she might return there.

Down by the Water

I took medication for the anxiety and for the cramping. I bled on everything. I bled for days. I went to see my mentor read at an event in downtown Seattle, probably too soon to safely have left the bed I had been confined to. I said nothing of the miscarriage. I wanted to pretend. I wanted to deny what had happened in my body. Brandon took me to see PJ Harvey at a big theater in SODO, another activity I refused to miss despite my condition. Instead I inched my body as close to the stage as I could. We embraced, held tightly to each other, as Polly Jean Harvey belted out the sultry, tortured lyrics of "To Bring You My Love" in her iconic, heavy voice.

But when she began to sing "Down by the Water," my legs went weak. I became dizzy. I braced myself against the soft whisper of her voice, against the words that I knew were coming. For a moment I was lost and alone. No matter Brandon's embrace, or the crowd around me, or even PJ Harvey herself just several heads away from me onstage, I was unreachable. Floating in a black sky, or a sea, or nothing, just those words in their hushed repetition.

PJ Harvey softly sang into the mic, "Little fish, big fish swimming in the water / Come back here and give me my daughter." She sang the words again and again and it felt like it was only to me, to the girl-shaped hole in my body. It's funny how things can take on new meanings. How we can twist and bend a phrase around our own broken hearts, like we're trying to suture the wounds. PJ Harvey whispered the words into the mic, like she knew the sting of them. I listened, alone in the dark lake my body had fallen into. Staring through hot tears, as they blurred the singer into a ghostly apparition.

The Riverbank

When I walked through the doors of my new home for the first time after the miscarriage, I was a ghost. I had somehow become spirit. I moved through the house in a fog, like if I tried I could move through walls. My body was still recovering, my mind was dulled in the metallic white haze of medication. I passed through the entryway, into the big living room, then the dining room. I stopped outside the room that was going to be the nursery but wouldn't look at it. I went upstairs to my bedroom instead.

I looked at the small altar I'd erected, the candles, the sage, the can of smoked salmon, the bundled cedar, and my great-grandmother's picture. I saw the gemstones and the shells. And then I saw the photo of her, the small

image in black and white. My Death Star. I lunged toward the altar and brought the whole thing down in one
crash. I hurled things across the room. One by one I listened to them smash and shatter. Then I collapsed onto
the floor weeping, my fingers covered in soot and beads of
blood from where the glass had broken my skin. I cried,
with my cheek against the hardwood floor. I cried myself
into exhaustion, until everything went dark.

Things stayed dark. For days I haunted my own house
like a specter. If people came, I believed they couldn't see
me. If I screamed they wouldn't hear me. An angry and
destructive ghost. I chased the medication I still needed
with a glass of whiskey each night. I slept days away. I
woke forgetting she was no longer in me, and the whole
process would repeat. It became harder and harder to get
out of bed. Convinced I was a ghost, I thought if I could
make it past the doorway to what was going to be her
room, I could be at peace. I could travel to the next world
where it might be light and warm. This took courage. I
wrapped myself in a blanket one day and rushed through
the house as if it were on fire. I made it past the room and
to the front door. Out in the yard I threw down the blanket and fell on it. I wasn't aware of the time, or even what
day it was. It was daytime, I knew that at least from the
color of the sky. The fresh air stirred me from the cocoon
I felt wrapped in. As I breathed it in I wondered if I was
being revived.

Then I rolled over onto my side and saw the four baby trees Brandon had planted as a housewarming gift. Deep-green Douglas firs that stood less than three feet tall when he'd put them in the ground. I had forgotten about them. In the afternoon light I gasped at their crimson needles. I ran to the closest one and touched it. The brittle needles crumbled and blew to the ground before I could even hold a branch. "No," I wailed in my yard. "No, no, no, no." Unaware of whether or not my neighbors were out, or if anyone could see me, I wrapped my arms around my knees, curled into a ball at the base of my dead trees, and cried.

That night I lay on the hardwood floor for what felt like hours. I stared up at the ceiling, hating my house. It was a mess. Clothes were piled in the corners of my room, and what little food I did try to eat littered the surface of my writing desk. I saw a small paper sack stuffed under an old tote bag. Inside was medication meant for my cat, who had been diagnosed with a bad UTI earlier that year. She had recovered, but I never got around to discarding the bag. Six small vials remained. I had no idea what cat pain meds would do, and I didn't care. I opened each one and took them one after the other, the bitter fluid a tiny shot on my tongue.

I got drowsy, then I drew a bath. I dropped a rose bath bomb from Lush into the tub. Then I added rose petals and cedar oil. In my haze I remembered the song I started writing the night Brandon and I had our terrible fight. It rolled off my tongue like a spell:

You said of my family we were cursed,
specifically the women sick.
Unable to be in my body I got into the bath instead
blood red with herbs and medicines
I am trying to fix it. I am trying to wash off
the sickness . . .

The drowsiness intensified in the heat of the bath. Steam curled around my knees up to my hands and face. I closed my eyes and felt euphoric. Then I felt cold, like the bathwater had chilled suddenly and left my skin in goose bumps. My eyelids grew heavy, my limbs turned to lead. I heard waves on a distant shore and felt dirt between my toes. I saw four white walls, one window, and a house, big and out of reach.

I crawled out of the tub, rose petals clinging to my skin. I fell into my bed and pulled the blankets up over me, wondering what would find me in sleep. When I woke I was changed. If I had been a ghost, the six little vials on my hardwood floor had exorcised me back into my body. Reentry was excruciating. Every nerve in my body was on fire, and I felt a terror like nothing I had ever known. I picked up each little vial. They were light and empty, like seashells. As I dropped them into the trash, I closed my eyes and saw my great-grandmother standing against the roaring ocean in Quinault. We had both wanted to die. The waves of darkness had come to swallow me, too, but like her, I took one hard step backward, back to land, away from that tide.

I ran to the bookshelf and pulled out the Aunt Susie book. Some unknown voice inside was calling me to read. Laid out across my floor on a blanket, I thumbed through the pages. I remembered my past dream, my bare feet stepping over roots and stones to the sink in the clearing. I remembered the old Indian woman's face staring back at me, and the cold rush of water as I dunked my face in. I called Manuela, my old roommate and good friend in Seattle. I knew her heart, her care. I knew she would one day be a mother and that she would understand this kind of grief. "I need to go to the Skagit River. Right now," I said. Manuela agreed to come with me and lovingly re-arranged her day. I called Richard too. My heart was still too bruised, too raw, to call Brandon. He hadn't woken up the night my body released our baby, and I had not forgiven him.

Manuela picked me up and we made the hour-and-a-half drive north, collecting Richard along the way. I had gathered the shards of cedar and other broken things from my altar and a Pendleton blanket. We drove out past the small towns along the Skagit, till finally we were far enough from civilization. We pulled off the road at an old boat launch, overgrown with brush and sword ferns. It was freezing and the river was high.

My plan was to immerse myself in the Skagit, but my friends were nervous. They searched the car for rope, for anything that might secure me. They feared I would drown, but what they didn't realize was that I already had, that this was my resuscitation ritual.

I stepped out of my clothes and shivered in the cold. My breath puffed out in gray, delicate shapes beyond my lips. I floated the things from my altar down the river. One by one I threw the candles, the cedar, the prenatal vitamins into the water. I watched them rush and swirl and disappear. The river moved fast and felt like ice against my toes. I took two shaky steps into the Skagit.

A long cedar branch hung just a foot ahead of me. "Don't go beyond that branch," they called out. But I just stepped forward again and again until I was waist-deep. I took a deep breath and looked up at the mountains, green and gray and enveloped in fog. I saw the towering cedars and the climbing firs. The river roared around me, its icy current biting at my skin. Then I let myself fall into it. I clutched a root from the bank in my fist and felt the water pull and tug me. Suspended beneath the surface, I felt the small twigs and debris from the river flow past me. I felt the water like hands as it tore things from me, things like darkness and grief. It took these things, and I let them go downriver. I felt like I did as a child in the longhouse, surrounded by people holding me up, unwilling to let me go. This river wouldn't let me disappear.

In the frozen current I thought about disappearing. When I was young my mother tried to go missing. She had relapsed back into drugs and alcohol and left for many days at a time. I watched as she struggled, as she beat against the darkness. As an adult, I tried to do the same thing. I tried to make myself disappear. It seemed like a strange coincidence, how often we put ourselves in danger. Beneath the surface of the river I thought about the times I spent running away from home, the places I slept, the nights my mother must have spent worried. I thought about the girl who had been growing in my own body, how my body had given up on her. Had she also disappeared? Then I remembered Brandon's diagnosis. In his anger, he had referred to the women in my family as sick. We all suffered some kind of sad sickness. I thought of my mother's relapse, the night my great-grandmother walked into the sea, and my own ocean, those little plastic syringes I thought would take me out of this world.

There was a reason I chose this place on the Skagit River. My great-grandmother lived up and down this river as a young woman. This river was where Aunt Susie trained to be a medicine worker, a healer. Aunt Susie was the first woman in our tribe to be trained in this kind of spiritual practice, the first woman Indian doctor. At ten years old her father brought her out here as part of her training. She removed her clothes and shoes, and the pebbles on the shore were so cold they froze to the soles of her feet. But this is how she learned to heal. If the women of my lineage were sick, were we also able to heal ourselves? Beneath the surface of the rushing river I saw Aunt Susie's words, translated from Lushootseed into English: "Out in the stream I floated in the pitch-black night. I was not afraid. Nothing was allowed to scare me. That is how I found this particular power, which always helps me, even as I grow older. The power sustains me, it tells me it shall be my strength."

I resurfaced gasping for air and shook the river water from my skin and hair as I ran to shore. My skin was beet red. It stung against the cold, and my friends brought me a towel and the Pendleton blanket. I patted my face dry, shivering in the cold air. Richard looked worried. "I'm gonna be okay now," I reassured him. I rubbed my hands together, their red color stark against the slate-gray sand.

"Yeah." Richard just looked down, hugged me, but then pulled back. His expression was more than worried; it was sad. It occurred to me that I had hurt him all over again. He had not recovered from the shock of finding out I was pregnant in the first place. I felt a weight when I stood there with him, one I couldn't bear. I couldn't prop him up; I couldn't help him through this hurt. I had been so lost in time with him. I hadn't considered what my time travel or my indecisiveness might do to him. All that time we spent together, listening to records, talking about what it was like when we were teenagers, living in the past, all of that vanished with the pregnancy. I had pulled away. He had become distant. And now I stepped back from him, too weak to let anyone lean on me. The ride home was quiet. I could feel myself missing him already, and the guilt that followed stung worse than the river water, but like the water it was necessary. It was something I needed to shed. He couldn't come with me on this journey, and though it was hard to face, I knew I needed to leave my childhood love behind.

—

When I got home, I rested. The next day my parents dropped in. They often stopped by and I didn't mind. They were thrilled to have me around the corner. Years ago they had moved into a house that had also been in the family for generations, just up the street. They would joke, "You haven't lived this close to us since you ran away at fourteen." It was true. I hadn't. I came downstairs as my dad's truck pulled up out front.

"We brought you a housewarming gift." He said it cheerfully. I smiled and rolled my eyes.

I protested that I didn't need a gift, that they'd already helped so much, but my dad was already loading in two massive paintings and a bentwood cedar box. The smile dropped from my face completely. I opened my mouth to speak, to tell them I couldn't accept these, but before I could, he was already propping them up against the walls.

"Your mom and I thought you should have these in your new home. Your uncle Ron's paintings and his box. We thought you could use them." I couldn't help the tears that formed in the corners of my eyes and brushed them away quickly. I hadn't told them about the miscarriage. I hadn't even told them about the pregnancy. The paintings were massive—they took up three walls in my living room. I stood in awe. How could my parents have known?

"I can't take these from you guys," I started to say, but my mom, who had come in with another painting, a small one, in her hand, interrupted me.

"Don't be silly, we still have a few at the house." She hugged me and I felt like collapsing into her arms like a child to cry and scream and tell her what I had just done in the river and why, but I didn't. I stayed quiet. I thanked them and said goodbye. I watched them leave, but I didn't feel alone, not anymore, not next to Uncle Ron's paintings.

I don't know why my parents decided to gift me the paintings. But here they were, now, in my home. I remembered my dream. I had dreamt of my great-grandmother my entire life. This made sense, I was her namesake. We were connected. But I had dreamt about my uncle only that one time. I remembered how excited I was to see him in my dream, how the hairs on my arms stood up in my uncle's presence. I hadn't known why at the time, but now I did. Because it wasn't a memory; it wasn't a dream. I had been in the presence of his spirit, and his spirit had traveled a long way to visit me that night. I was beginning to understand why.

Sitting in my living room with the paintings, I felt a shiver, like breath on my neck or fingers in my hair. I studied the faces on the canvases, marked in paint, the drums, and the thick, billowing smoke. This power had been with me the whole time. This ability to heal, to mend, to find strength—I had access to it. Looking up at the dancers, I was reminded of something. Somewhere close to where I took my plunge, the river forks and there is a small creek. This is a place that the people considered sacred, a place they went to bathe and cleanse their spirits, and it was near this creek that they used to gather the red paint.

Point Defiance

When summer came, I was stronger. I was healing. I was
ready to throw a housewarming party. I walked up and
down the streets behind my house picking blackberries.
I filled a metal mixing bowl to the brim with juicy berries, listening to Crass through my headphones. The land
looked different than in the time of my ancestors. There
were broken-down cars and the occasional boarded-up
house. A giant casino obstructed the view, and the river
was polluted, but you could still see the mountain and the
Salish Sea. You could still fill a bowl full of berries and
make a pie for your guests.

I invited Richard to the party and when he said he
couldn't make it, my heart stung small and slight. I had
known he would decline. Months had passed since the

miscarriage, but he was still healing. So was I. Healing is different than self-medicating. Healing is exhausting. Stepping out from behind the veil had not been easy. Instead of occupying the delicious haze of denial, I now stood in the blinding light of what I had become. I had been so evasive, so afraid, and it began long before the miscarriage. I had to face the ways I had learned to self-medicate. I had spent my life until this point searching for a permanent home. I looked for it in abandoned buildings, in friends and lovers. I looked for it in pills and alcohol. I looked for it in a marriage neither Brandon nor I had been ready for.

A lot of friends showed up. Kids ran along my deck wielding sparklers, and adults shot BB guns and played punk records. It was a celebratory night. Near dusk a group of friends approached me, led by Taryn, a woman I had seen for many years at different DIY shows. She was super active in the scene, had been in multiple bands, and was constantly working on something new. Taryn intimidated me in a way I admired. She was strong, blunt, and fearless. With a couple of other friends, she presented me with a housewarming gift: a large abalone shell, hand-dipped candles, a vial of honey, and one vivid, shimmering blue jay feather. The beauty of the gift rendered me speechless, and I listened as Taryn and several other friends invited me to join their band.

"We've read your stuff and know you're a poet,"

Taryn went on to explain, "and we really want to incorporate your voice into our new project, Medusa Stare." I could have cried. But instead, I thanked them for the beautiful gift and for coming to the party and said hell yes to joining Medusa Stare. I sent them home with a couple of zines, feeling giddy and stupid, like a kid before Christmas.

I had invited Brandon. We made nervous conversation throughout the party, both of our hearts still broken from the loss of our marriage and the loss of our unborn child. We were stuck together somehow, drawn to each other out of habit and heartache. Brandon stayed late. He helped pick up as I did the dishes in the kitchen. A massive sadness overwhelmed me as I patted the dishes dry and listened to him one room over. This was the life we had wanted, wasn't it? Husband and wife. Entertaining friends, having guests in our permanent home. He slept over. Though we were intimate, I couldn't escape the sadness. That night led to more nights. Soon he was coming down a couple of times a week until finally he asked me something. He didn't want to simply continue dating me. He wanted something real.

"I want you to sign the papers." He was serious and stoic in his asking. My heartbeat sped up. "I can't do this half-assed anymore. I want us to try again. I want you to sign the papers."

We had never actually signed the marriage certificate.

We had been married in the eyes of my culture—the blanket ceremony had bound us—but not in the eyes of the state. Applying for the marriage license had been on Brandon's list of pre-wedding tasks, and he had not done it. At the time I had shrugged it off. I didn't think I cared about a piece of paper. Had I really not cared? I wasn't sure. It had been a lifetime ago. But now he stood before me, asking me for something he needed. I knew I couldn't sign those papers. I cried. We argued, and he left angry. I promised him I'd think about it.

We drove to the beach on a hot August morning. We stumbled upon an old boat launch by the train tracks with a view of Point Defiance Park and the Tacoma Narrows Bridge. Even on a hot summer day, the seawater was frigid and we only dipped our feet in. "It wasn't right for me to fall in love with Richard when I still loved you," I said.

"Yeah, no shit." Brandon still resented me. He was angry. He had every right to be.

"I wasn't okay." I was trying to explain the ways I had been wrong, and it wasn't easy.

He shifted his weight on the concrete boat launch. "I don't want to continue to see you. If you don't want to really try . . ." He trailed off, but I knew what he meant. I knew he wanted me to be his wife. My heart sank. I had wanted that for so long, nearly a decade. I had wanted to be grounded, to feel rooted and safe. It is an important thing, to feel safe. Safety was something I'd chased since childhood, the reservation, the assaults. I ran away to try to find it. I put myself in danger in the hopes of finding it. And enough was enough. Ever since Australia I had been unwilling to try, but instead of feeling guilty for that I began to understand it. My trust and my safety had been compromised and I could not recover. This idea of a permanent home had been too important to me, and I'd let it consume me. I knew what I had to do. I felt my whole body engage, felt every muscle and nerve when I said it. It felt like an act of treason, like my heart was defying something my mind wanted. I loved him. And I had to let him go.

"I'm not well." I lowered my eyes to the seaweed suspended in the blue water beneath our feet. "I need to get better." I didn't know what better looked like. I didn't have a clear plan or even an idea. I just knew I had been doing something wrong for so long. I knew I needed a change.

That night I sat in my house alone, cross-legged on the floor of my room. Spread out in front of me were books and paperwork. I needed to finish grad school and continue searching for something I had not found in a home or in a marriage. The information fanned out in front of me was laid out like a map. Comptia, Aunt Susie, and taqʷšəblu—these women were my guides, my lighthouses burning in the distance.

My great-grandmother had gifted me her name, and

in doing so she gave me an identity and a purpose. Aunt Susie had guided my great-grandmother; perhaps she had given her the same purpose. Imbedded within us was the mapwork of how to heal. We had the tools to mend what had been broken, to replace what was taken.

I saw now that my search for a permanent home was a step along a more important path. The map that I had strewn across my floor was made of texts, old photos, and books about our tribe. In it I saw that my path pointed toward a small fishing village on the southern coast of Washington, where the mouth of the Columbia River opened up to the sea, separating Oregon and Washington. I was going to drive to the Chinook region, where Comptia was born, the place that would become the Astoria Trading Post. I was going to see the house that the captain had built on her land. I was going to Ilwaco.

Deadman's Cove

Goonies never say "die." I thought about this as I crested the Astoria Bridge. A thick gray fog enveloped my car, the seafoam-green metal of the bridge appearing and disappearing. As I came down the other side, Astoria came into view. Goonies never say "die." But Goonies never had to say "colonization" or "relocation" or "smallpox." I crossed the large mouth of the Columbia River, the place where the river met the sea. I was on my own treasure hunt, but I wasn't looking for gold. I was looking for answers.

My room at the Riverwalk Inn was small and cozy against the dark afternoon. A drizzle slid down the windows as I read family histories and letters, wrapped in my grandmother's wool shawl. I burned sage. The place beyond the window felt charged, connected to me in some way I couldn't name.

Pan, my dog, needed a walk, so I ventured out into the town. Astoria was cute. Quaint storefronts promised handcrafted art, nautical-themed wall hangings, knits, and things made with shells. I passed by the shops and breweries along the wet wood of the boardwalk. Pan obsessed over the lingering scent on a urine-soaked planter box. I left her to it, looping her leash around a bike rack before popping into the Gypsy Treasure Chest, a shop claiming to house curios, gemstones, Wiccan spell books, and all things spiritual. Inside I found only kitschy gifts, imported jewelry, belly dance costumes, tumbled rocks, and tarot cards. I eyed the decks on display. The Faerie Oracle Deck, the Goddess Deck. I rolled my eyes when I found it: Native American Medicine Cards. The deck featured a painted wolf circled within a dream catcher on the cover, and aside from my own reflection in my bathroom's fluorescent-lit mirror, it was my first native sighting since arriving in Astoria. I turned the box over and read the contents: Raven, Bear, Badger, and Coyote. Spirit animals all representing different omens. This one means financial stress, this one means emotional blocks, this one means distress, and so on. Neither the artist nor the creator of the medicine deck were native. I felt annoyed, but worse than that I felt lonely. After purchasing a small vial of rose oil, I thanked the silver-haired white man wearing a turquoise ring and left.

Pan stopped at a patch of grass on a corner. As she walked circles in the small park I looked out across the water. Ilwaco was somewhere out there, past the beach and through the trees. Tucked somewhere along that coast was the small fishing village my ancestor called home.

　After dinner I watched *The Goonies* in my hotel room. I watched the film not as research but in an attempt to cheer myself up on this lonely trip down the coast. I tried to enjoy the "Truffle Shuffle," the "Baby Ruth," and the "Slick Shoes." I couldn't help but wonder why there wasn't a Chinook Goonie. Shouldn't there be? I amused myself with visions of my Chinook Goonie, with braids and the ability to catch a salmon. But there was no Chinook character in *The Goonies*. Not even a background character. The story took place here, on Chinook land, yet my Indigenous ancestors were invisible. I went to bed worried about what I might find in Ilwaco. With Pan curled against my feet on the oversized hotel bed, I dreamt of tidal waves, canoes crashing against the rocks, and the great bodies of whales slamming into my hotel window.

I woke early and downed a cup of hotel coffee. Pan and I hit the road as the sun rose over a glittering Columbia River. Victorian houses dotted the hills and cliffsides overlooking the water. Almost every house in Astoria was

Victorian, with wraparound porches and rooftops decorated with ornate carvings. I thought they looked like toy
houses, doll houses, something made-up and pretend. I
closed my eyes at a stoplight and tried to imagine the land
here before the ships came, before the settlers made Astoria what it was, quaint, beautiful, and white.

I drove through the town of Chinook on my way to
Ilwaco and pulled off the road at the first "Heritage Site"
I encountered. It was an unimpressive patch of land with
a few rickety picnic tables dotting the tree line. I let Pan
off leash and walked to the edge of the park. Through the
trees I stood in awe of the coastal beauty. The tree line
gave way to a sparse and rocky shore. Gray stones, crawl-
ing waves, and the long branches of trees sweeping over
the beach like hands. This was my favorite of nature's
intersections, the forest and the sea. To see windswept
coastal trees, jagged rocks, and crashing waves ignited
something in me. It always felt like a memory. It felt like
home.

Pan sniffed around the base of a wooden sign. The
painted placard told of a certain kind of seabird. A big
and beautiful creature that called this coastline home. I
looked up from reading, in a silly moment of hoping that
I might spot one circling. Returning to the text, I read
on to discover that this particular shore was where Captain "Whoever" first spotted these massive birds from his
ship off the coast. The rocky shoreline was treacherous,

but the placard honored the seamen for their bravery, for maneuvering their boats carefully to shore. This site was noted for being a favored hunting ground for these prized birds. I watched my dog take a shit in the wet grass. I didn't pick it up.

The next site I encountered was Fort Columbia on the river. A sign in the parking lot informed me that if I didn't pay for a day pass I would receive a big fine. I parked and didn't pay. If a park ranger stopped a Coast Salish girl and her dog wandering the sites of the first settlement on her peoples' land, would he really give her a fine? I was sure he would, but I wanted the chance to challenge it anyway. To my disappointment we wandered the abandoned fort undisturbed.

It was a bust. Just a bunch of sterile wooden buildings old and empty. Historical facts printed on signs faded by the sun. The white men who once lived here were barbers, musicians, and farmers, not only soldiers. This was a "community." On my way out I stopped at the massive wooden sign hanging close to the entrance. In bold letters it read, FORT COLUMBIA: HERE WAS THE HOME OF THE CHINOOK INDIANS AND THEIR GREAT CHIEF, COMCOMLY.

Was. The word caught in my throat like a cough, like something you try to swallow. *They once lived here.* That was the only information about my ancestors provided in the large park and all its preserved buildings, its old guns and bunkers. Just thirteen words. That's all they could spare. The Chinook people did not have some wild adventure like the Goonies. There was no fantastic and quirky way to save their beloved home. There was no cave of whimsical booby traps or skeleton pianos to conquer. No pirate ship loaded with gold would keep them here.

There wasn't much to the town of Ilwaco. A couple of tourist shops, a fish-and-chips place, a cannery. The heritage museum was run by an ancient white woman. She smiled when she greeted me, gave me a walking map of Ilwaco, and left me to wander the corridors and the rooms of the small museum. I saw sepia-toned portraits of Chinook people, canoes, and paintings of plank houses. A young woman in a portrait behind glass wore an almost identical pair of dentalium shell earrings to the ones that I had on that day. I ran my fingertips along the delicate ends of the white shells, down to the antique beads, and traced the glass where the woman's earrings hung. *We wear them because we are loved.* Tania's words echoed in my head.

I visited the town's small library next. There I discovered that Comptia and Capt. James Johnson were considered the first family of Ilwaco. In an old historical society's reference book, I learned the captain had died at sea. That's all it said: Capt. James Johnson died at sea. Next I read about a place called Deadman's Cove. I knew I had to go.

The trail that cut through the woods and along the coastline was covered in moss and wet stones. The consistently damp earth smelled like home. Pan and I made our way toward the scenic lookout. Tourists passed us along the way, smiling and saying things like "What a pretty dog" and "It's a beautiful day." Couples hiking together hurried by. Families with children on smartphones took up too much space on the trail. I smirked at the sight of hikers loaded down with heavy packs, CamelBaks of water, and special hiking sticks. Such gear was unnecessary. It was just a trail, maintained and well kept.

Through the density of the forest came the sound of waves against rocks. Pan and I quickened our pace. The tree line opened up and revealed a steep cliffside. Beneath the drop-off waves roared against massive black rocks jutting out from the blue depths of the cove. Deadman's Cove was picturesque. The water a dark, clean, blue. Sword ferns and trees grew along the climbing stones. The water raged, sending tall waves and sprays of seafoam into the trees.

This part of the coast, where the Columbia meets the ocean, is known as the Graveyard of the Pacific. Over two thousand ships have gone under here. Beneath the beauty of the surface lie pile upon pile of wrecked ships. A cemetery of drowned men, decaying boats, nameless explorers.

Perhaps this was where the captain met his demise.

Right here in Deadman's Cove. I watched the ocean beat itself against the beach and said a silent thank-you. Perhaps the ocean had been looking out for my ancestors, as it claimed one ship after another. Perhaps it was trying to keep them safe. The men who sailed here brought disease and gold and alcohol. They brought treaties and names for places already named. They crossed an ocean to climb these shores, and the water pulled them under when it could, to keep the land as it was, even if only for a moment longer. I paid my respects not to the men lost at sea but to the sea itself, the power beneath the waves.

Elwahco

I woke up in the clean white sheets of the bed in my room at the Riverwalk Inn. My dog was turning circles in front of the bed. The pale gray light of a northwest morning came in through the window, and Pan turned another circle. She had to go out. I rolled out of bed and slipped my boots on. I let her do her business on the manicured lawn in front of the hotel while I stood in sweatpants and a denim jacket.

In the lobby I had a terrible cup of complimentary coffee and a bowl of granola with almond milk. I watched a scattering of strangers start their day. An older man read the paper by a big window. A young couple decked out head to toe in North Face and REI outdoor wear giggled and discussed their upcoming adventures for the day. A married couple bickered over the distance of their next drive as they fussed over a sleeping toddler. I breathed a sigh of relief, happy to be on my own for the first time in a long time. A kind of peace washed over me, and I collected my things and stepped out into the misty drizzle. Today I would go to the place where Comptia Koholowish had lived. I drove over the bridge again, past the fort and the first missionary church, and into the small town of Ilwaco. I had read that the town was named after Elwahco Jim, the son of Chief Comcomly and someone who was remarked to be a "friendly Indian guide to the settlers." I thought of Elwahco Jim each time I passed a street called Johnson. Everything in the area was named after the settlers, everything except the place itself.

When I arrived at 124 Lake Street the sun had broken through the clouds. Everything previously covered in rain now glittered in the new sunlight. I parked my car and stepped onto the wet pavement. I had many times imagined the house where my ancestor once lived. I suppose I thought it would be bigger. I studied the white house before me, the way the wood creaked and whined, the smell of cut grass and asphalt. I closed my eyes and saw Comptia weaving, saw her gutting a fish, cleaning a salmon. I saw her harvesting berries, nettles, and camas. I saw her gathering the things she would prepare and feed her family. I saw her holding a large cedar basket and singing. But this was not my life. Not the white house made of wood, not the picket fence or the porch that wraps around, not the ocean roaring somewhere beyond the trees or the salt in the air. None of this belonged to me.

My eyes opened to the glaring sunlight. I looked to the lime-green plastic chair on the porch, the American flag waving in the breeze, and the bronze placard in the white wood stating that this home was of historical significance. I remembered to come back to my own time, to today, to right now.

It had taken me so long to get here.

I sat down and lit a candle. I placed a bundle of cedar on the concrete. In my hands I rolled a piece of red clay I had found on the beach earlier. I felt it dust my fingertips. I was trying to heal. I was trying to honor her, to say, *I know you were here and that you were brave.*

I hate the word "brave." Like I hate "victim," "survivor," or "squaw." I was tired of the names white people had given us. Jane was my ancestor's English name. Did she forget her Chinook name? Her Indian name? Did the English erase it? Did she forget she was called Comptia long before she was ever called Jane, or Indian, or Wife, or Mother?

I was tired of being brave. I would rather be something else. Carefree? An aging millennial. Someone who enjoys listening to the Cranberries and Cyndi Lauper on road trips down the coast. Call me a writer. Call me a riot grrrl. Call me Coast Salish or poet. Call me a girl who loves Nick Cave, and night swimming, and ramen, and old Bikini Kill records. I no longer wish to be called resilient. Call me reckless, impatient, and emotional. Even Indigenous. Call me anything other than survivor. I am so many more things than brave.

The house seemed like a ghost of its former self. It felt like someplace I had been before but no longer recognized. Like a switchback trail you've been down a thousand times, transformed with the seasons. You have to second-guess yourself against the changing flora. You have to wonder, *Have I been here before?*

It must have been so beautiful in its day. The pointed roof, the wraparound porch, leaded windows, all of it so grandiose considering the time of its construction. In the mid-1800s this place must have seemed like a palace. I closed my eyes and again saw a woman alone in the cold. Not allowed in the big house. I saw her saying goodbye to her children each morning. I saw her speaking her traditional language to no one. As I performed my ritual I wasn't scared of whoever lived here now. *So what if they come out?* I thought. Maybe they will be the worst kind of small-town people, the kind with guns and Make America Great Again hats. If they ask me what I am doing here, I won't answer, because I don't know. I had been wondering about this place since childhood, and I was exhausted. The sound of the front door opening startled me from my thoughts and brought me back to the house, the sidewalk, the yard. I didn't move.

The man who lived at 124 Lake Street came out the front door smiling. "Go ahead and take a picture," he laughed. "It's a free country." An interesting choice of words, I thought. I stepped back as I often do when men approach me but forced a smile and extended my hand in introduction. I asked about the owner. I explained that I had been to the heritage museum in town and that they had given me a walking-tour map that featured the house. I was doing research for a book, I said.

Next to the historical reference regarding the house on Lake Street was a bit of information I hadn't seen yet. It stated that "the Johnson house was built by Captain Johnson, a sea captain, who with his wife later drowned at sea. An heir asked to have the house condemned; fortunately it was never torn down." Comptia did not drown at sea. Her cause of death is unknown, but she died on land at the age of thirty-five. The women in my family believe she died of a broken heart. She had been forced to live alone, without her people, her ways, her freedom for too long. Her body and her spirit chose to leave this world, yet this pamphlet prescribed her the same fate as the Scottish man who married her. She was not even allowed her own death. I was irritated by this misinformation. The second statement also made me angry. An heir had asked for the property to be condemned. *Why shouldn't it be?* I wondered. Tear it down and in its place erect a carving of Comptia.

The polite white man stood before me, talking about the renovations of the house. He evaded giving me the names of the current owners and instead briefly explained that he had lived here in the 1980s. I thought about his cheerful statement: Of course you can take a photo of the house. *It's a free country.* It hasn't always been.

"My ancestor lived here." I tried to offer more of an explanation as to why I was standing in front of his former home taking pictures and burning cedar, but nothing came out. He didn't seem to mind or even take note of my interest. Perhaps he gets this a lot. Perhaps he thought I was on one of those haunted tours, and maybe I was. I was looking for ghosts.

"Is there by chance a small shed on the property?" I found the nerve to ask. "An original structure, still here?"

"Oh, sure," the man beamed, delighted to divulge the facts he did know about the property. "Right around here," he waved me around the corner of the house and pointed. "It's the original carriage house. Built in the 1800s." He lit up when he said it, proud of this piece of settler history. *The carriage house?* My lips trembled before falling open. I wanted to correct him, to tell him that the structure housed more than carriages and old wagon wheels, that it housed my ancestor, that a woman lived here, but before I could speak the man waved a friendly goodbye, said something about needing to pick up his daughter, and disappeared.

I stood in front of the small white shed. The lone window was a black pool of glass against the sunlight. I stepped closer and found a woman looking back at me, floating there in the window. Trapped within four walls. My throat felt gripped by something, crushed and aching. My stomach tied itself into knots and my limbs felt weak.

Comptia Koholowish stood in the square of glass, framed in the window. Her dark hair fell past her shoulders. Her eyes, a deep brown, stared back at me. She wasn't smiling, but she wasn't sad either. She was something else. Strong. She hadn't been rescued, or saved; she had survived. I swallowed hard and stared into the window, into my own reflection. *You come from a long line of strength*, my mother used to say. *It's in your blood.* I took a deep breath. I gave myself permission to walk away, to release myself from pain. I thought I had come for her, but she had called me there, to tell me something. It wasn't to say a prayer for her, or to honor her, or to release her. She was releasing me. I looked through the glass and saw my own prison. Then I saw the walls fall down. No one kept me there, no one built walls around me, or caged me, or held me back. Comptia Koholowish gave me permission to leave, to finally walk away. I turned my back to the shed and took my first few steps away from it, in her honor.

Before I reached the edge of the yard I knelt down to the grass. I still had a small bit of red clay in the palm of my hand. I rolled it in my fist once more and placed it on the wet earth. A smile crept onto my face, a small and delicate gratitude. Maybe I wasn't going to be a wife or a mother. I didn't know what I was going to be, but I had the strength to walk away and toward something else, toward whatever I wanted.

My family comes from red paint. We have always had the ability to heal. Healing is different than self-medicating. Healing takes more strength. I would never dance in the longhouse, but I come from dancers, and that strength helps me every day. I climbed back into my car and headed north. Before I pulled onto the highway that would take me home, I caught my reflection in the rearview mirror. I had touched my face while brushing a hair from my eyes. My finger left a small streak of red paint along my cheekbone. I smiled when I saw it there. I didn't wipe it away.

hədiw II

I was leaving in one week, to drive cross-country in a van with my band. But I needed permission first. That's what led me here to my parents' home, to this table where I sat with my father awaiting my mother's return. To the side of the table was a large painting done by my uncle. In the painting a figure stands in the center of a longhouse, surrounded by dancers and drums. The figure is adorned in a cedar woven headdress, and on his face is deep-red paint. One detail always struck me hardest: that red paint across their faces.

My dad looked at me from across the table. He knew how hard this year had been on me. "You're powerful, you're strong, and you deserve *good* things." His voice shook a little when the words came. "You deserve love,

Sasha." I had forgotten that somewhere along the way. I smiled and pushed the images of my younger and angrier self out of my mind. I tried not to think about the child me with a shaved head and black lipstick, climbing out of the small square window of our single-wide trailer, running away again in the dead of night, to escape the reservation, the trailer, our life. I tried not to think of younger me hitchhiking two towns over, fourteen and afraid, but not too afraid to crawl into the cab of a stranger's truck. I had put my parents through so much.

I had asked to wear the paint before, years ago, while marching with the Two Spirit flag at the pride parade. Some of the other people who marched with us wore their regalia; I thought it might be appropriate. It wasn't. My mother had scolded me and explained that the paint wasn't for that. It wasn't an adornment. I worried I might have crossed a line again.

My mom returned with a bag of cedar shavings and a small chunk of red clay.

Her eyes were wet as she set the items down on the table in front of me. "I've been waiting a long time to give this to you."

White people might call it magic, or witchcraft. Anthropologists might call it religion. But what happened in the longhouse was spirit power and, in its presence, I felt something move in me. When I was small, I was afraid of the dancers inside the longhouse. I minded the instructions from my elders. I did not look the dancers in the eye as they passed by. As my great-grandmother's namesake, I carried a responsibility. Perhaps this is why she thought it important to take me inside the longhouse when I was so young. She wanted to teach me something. She held my small hand in hers. As the smoke stung my eyes, as the cedar burned and the shadows moved silhouetted against the flames, I sat afraid and brave at the same time. The pounding drums, the songs, the orange flames, and all that smoke enveloped me in a kind of dream. The dancers moved like shadows and I had to work hard to obey, when all I wanted was to look, was to know what would happen if one of these strangers, one of these dancers, caught my gaze. Something rose in me when the dancers with red paint came close.

One time I tugged at my mother's sleeve inside the longhouse, "What does the red paint mean?"

"The red paint is for the healers," my mother pulled the drooping blanket back up to my shoulders.

I come from a long line of dancers who wore red paint. They were the healers. The medicine workers. I didn't understand that when I was little. I only understood the power of the longhouse. The work that happened within its walls was secret, known only to the families present. The songs weren't sung outside of this place. The dances were reserved only for this fire and its smoke in the winter. That first night in the longhouse locked the smell of smoke in my hair and it clung to my clothes. "Ewww," I remember one girl in my class saying as she sat behind me, "someone smells like campfire." And she plugged her nose, shook her golden head back and forth, and wafted the air away dramatically. I did smell like campfire. The smell of campfire, dirt, and sometimes smoked fish seeped into my clothes. Our neighbor smoked salmon on the property, and the smoke seemed to permeate everything. But that morning the girl's upturned nose couldn't bother me. I wouldn't let it. I huffed my hair and smelled the power in it, and it felt like something that truly belonged to me.

Now, sitting at my mother's table, I rolled the chunk of red clay around in my fingertips.

I watched as it dusted them pink. I closed my fist around it, the fragile power of healing that belonged to me. Strength is a strange feeling when it is new, like something that can crumble. I held mine soft and delicate. I welcomed it.

Hu-dee-ew . . .

Epilogue:
Spirit Dancing

Before leaving on tour with Medusa Stare, I had one last thing to do. One last rite needed to be performed before I began this new journey. On my child's due date, the child who would never be born, I went to the coast. I asked my mom how to properly do a burning. I was instructed on how to make the fire and the food, and at sunset I set out for the beach. A woman I loved came with me. Marguerite was the woman I'd dated outside my marriage, and we remained friends. She didn't want me to do it alone. We made a big meal of baked salmon, roasted vegetables, and bread. In a bag I gathered all the things I had collected for my baby: the first and only photo I had of her, when she was just a Death Star, a stuffed blue whale I bought in Hawaii, and a stuffed rabbit gifted to me by Brandon's mother. Over a crackling fire made of cedarwood, I placed a plate piled with food. I wept as the flames swallowed the only meal I'd ever cook for her. Then I burned things. Prenatal vitamins, the stuffed animals, the *What to Expect When You're Expecting* book. I tore it page by page and fed the fire. I cried, and the fire eventually shrank. I had nothing else to feed it. As I watched the embers glow, my knees went weak and all the hairs on the back of my neck stood up. I felt the presence of the spirit world close. I looked out at the massive waves rolling in the distance and the piles of driftwood around us. The beach was dark, moonlit. I took a deep breath and closed my eyes. I saw my uncle at the edge of the water. I saw him in his longhouse regalia, face covered in red paint. I gasped. Behind him I saw other figures, other dancers, but it was him in front. He was coming to take her. I let out a cry of grief and relief as I felt her go. I felt her leave my spirit. She had not been ready to leave that day at the river, but now she was. Waves pounded the shore heavy and loud, crashing like drums in ceremony. I sat kneeling at the last glowing coals of the fire, and all around me was a song.

The next morning, Marguerite and I had breakfast and took photos at an abandoned school. At a grocery store, a woman with a screaming baby stood frantic and tired in front of us. "Breeders," Marguerite whispered in my ear. "Hey, at least that's not you." And I burst into laughter. We laughed hard and loud all the way out to the car. It felt good to finally laugh again, and I loved her for it. It was good to feel light again. We drove back to the city with a cheerfulness I hadn't known in months.

After my mother gave me the red paint, I tucked it into a small woven bag and took it on tour with me, along with the cedar shavings from the carving of the Maiden of Deception Pass. These were my talismans. I didn't need them for protection. I carried them with me for strength. The red paint came from the creek off the Skagit, the sacred place where my ancestors bathed in ritual. And the Maiden of Deception Pass had been my favorite Salish story as a child. She was strong, fearless, and saved her people from starvation by marrying the sea. Once a year she came back to land to visit her people, fulfilling a promise she had made, but as the years went on, she became more and more ocean-like. Until one year, she stood on shore, covered in shells and seaweed, finding it difficult to breathe, and her people released her from her promise. She never came to shore again; instead, her people were comforted by the pieces of kelp floating on the surface, convinced this was the maiden's hair. My great-grandmother had been at the unveiling of the massive carving of the maiden. It still stands on the beach at the pass. The cedar shavings I carry with me had been gifted to my family the day of the unveiling. My great-grandmother had worn a cedar woven dress and told stories in the traditional language. This was before I was born. The cedar shavings carried that day with me and the strength of both my great-grandmother and the sea maiden.

With my red paint packed, along with three inhalers, too many punk shirts, and a sleeping bag, I was ready for tour. We piled in the van and drove through the night, toward our first show in Minneapolis. I woke up at a truck stop in Idaho, then again as we crossed the state line into Montana. This was different than being on tour with Brandon's band. This van felt like family. We told stories, we joked and laughed and took pictures of one another. We listened to Janet Jackson and sang every word to "Escapade."

The van broke down just outside of Butte, Montana. Even this didn't take away the magic I felt being on tour. I wasn't with Brandon. I wasn't with Richard. This was our van—mine and my bandmates'. I watched our drummer tinker with something under the hood. I looked out and saw Lito, our guitar player, pacing back and forth in the hot sun holding their phone up searching for signal. "Do you think they have Lyft out here?" We all laughed.

The tow truck arrived and shuttled us in groups to a nearby garage. I bought a bag of pita chips and some hummus from the market next door and sat down on the curb with my book. I was reading a book about Coast Salish spirit dancing, written by a woman who knew my great-grandmother. She studied the religion and spiritual practices of the Coast Salish people in the seventies. I read about fasting, and spirit quests, and the dances that happened in the longhouse. In the middle of the book was a spread of photographs. The first two were of my great-great-grandparents. My great-great-grandmother is posing for the camera in a small, black-and-white photo. The caption reads, "Louise Anderson in her red paint cedar bark headdress." I ran my fingers along the tattered page. Her face was pointed right up at me, into the lens, unapologetically strong. With permission from my parents, I wore red paint when I performed with Medusa Stare. It was my own ceremony, my way to honor my ancestors and myself. I would never dance in the longhouse, but I would find my own ritual of healing. When I wore the red paint it was for the wounds we carried in our bodies, through generations. It was for the sadness we battled, the addictions we fought. It was for the grief of losing our land, our bodies, our language, and our children. It was for the violence we faced, being torn from our homes, surviving epidemics and assaults. The red paint was to remind me of where I came from. I was not a weak person. I was not a victim or a person whose trauma ruled them. If the women of my family were sick, we knew how to heal. That's who we were, and medicine was in our blood.

The van was fixed, and before the sun went down we were back on the road to Minneapolis. We arrived for our first show just before nightfall and tumbled out of the van with our bags and all of our equipment. The venue was crowded and rowdy. I snuck into a cramped bathroom and placed the red paint and the bundle of cedar on the counter like on an altar.

The bathroom mirror was covered in punk stickers and graffiti, marked by the bands that had come before. People shouted as guitars tuned. An occasional airplane flew overhead, and I heard people laugh as they funneled down the stairway into the show space. I stared back at the mirror. Face forward. Face painted. Face marked by grief, by trauma, by loss, and by generations of violence. The muscle memory of survival coursed through me, and this face looked back at me asking me one thing: *Did I deserve to wear it?*

I saw Comptia. I saw my mother, her mother, and her mother's mother. Out onstage our first song ended, and that was my cue to step forward. I gripped the mic with both hands and the crowd looked right at me. People with mohawks, with suicide chains and leather harnesses, with shirts that said things like THE FUTURE IS FEMME and YOU'RE ON STOLEN LAND, people with shaved heads and blue hair, people who were not afraid to be

quiet and listen looked back at me. I stared ahead into the
faces of strangers and spoke:

You said of my family
we were cursed
specifically the women
sick
unable to be in my body
I got into the bath instead
blood red with herbs and medicine
I am trying to fix it
I am trying to wash off
the sickness
you said of my ancestry
affliction
you said broken

like our wedding night
I am trying to fight it
I am drowning in it
this need
to fix it

to make myself
more white not just pale
but lilium
that delicate shade

of maiden less red
you said it was
my mother and grandmother's doing
said it was them who
made the men in my family
death hungry
it's true you knew the stories
my grandfather how he wandered
the wood at sunset
seeking ghosts
a generation later
my father wanders Tacoma
reaches the hospital
pleading to them I'm dying
at my wife's broken heart

that sad part of her
that is killing me

of the women I come from
you said damaged
said historically
said intergenerationally

from the red bathwater
I am remembering raccoons
their small paws curled into fists

how my mother must have seen
but didn't miss
didn't hit the brakes
didn't even try to
instead my brothers
heard the thuds of their
bodies beneath tires
as my mother said nothing
but continued
driving

you said of my family
we were sick
specifically the women
suffered something
unnameable
quiet sickness
opiate numb
my mother was only trying
to dull the pain
that had been gifted to her by blood
red I am less white beneath my skin
unforgiven by you fooled into
thinking I was something else

of my face your mother said
didn't look Indian what then

where do I keep it
if not on the skin
slice me open
like a persimmon
watch blood pour
out ribboning red
here is where I keep
seeds

in my DNA you'll find a catalog
a bouquet of heirlooms coursing
written inside my body a history

drink me and see
the morning my grandmother
walked into the sea

drink and see me below a
stranger and thrashing see red
party cups ringing my head in
halo

see me bent over
white powder and smiling
fist full of pills metallic
on my tongue and see how I turn off
like clockwork

this numb is what
we gather now what we
hold in our baskets how
we keep coming back
for it
like canned fish
thimbleberries
and hops picked
in summer

of the women of my family
you said addiction
said submission
from the red bath
I wrap a towel
around my nakedness
bergamot and rose petal
still clinging
to my breasts
set the cedar
down carefully
and step
to the mirror
to the face
looking back
as it says
shape-shift says

shake this
off or wilt
a pale tulip

tossed at his feet

ACKNOWLEDGMENTS

To my incredible parents, thank you for your blessing, your guidance along the way, and for believing I could do this work. Thank you for putting up with the hard times, the shaved head, blue hair dye, and running-away years. Thanks to my incredible mother and the wonderful folks at the Lushootseed Research Program for always helping me with my words, and to Zalmai Ɂəswəli Zahir for the translations. Thank you to Pamela Amoss for the work she did with my relatives in her book, *Coast Salish Spirit Dancing*. Thank you to my great-grandmother's friends and adopted family, Janet Yoder and Carolyn Michael, for always regaling me with the beautiful stories of the friendship you shared with my namesake.

Thank you to my small but fierce community of

fellow writers for reading and listening, for gushing guts with me and for holding me up. Thank you, Rob Hanna, for all those red marks on early drafts of my work, and for asking me what my story was. Thank you to the mentors I had along the way. Melissa Febos, thank you for telling me I had more to say and for the really cool playlists.

I want to thank my editor Harry at Counterpoint for holding my story delicately, for believing in it fiercely. Thank you to my amazing agent Duvall at Aragi for truly understanding my voice, for seeing something in me. And for the phone calls early in the morning after late nights of band practice. Thank you for pushing me, for making me laugh, and for totally understanding my love of nineties music.

I want to thank the folks at The Institute of American Indian Arts MFA program for helping me craft my many feelings into words. Thank you to the organizations who helped fund my trips down the coast while I researched. I want to acknowledge Seattle Artist Trust, Tacoma Artist Initiative Program, and Seattle Office of Arts for giving me opportunities to explore this project deeper.

I want to express a deep gratitude for all of my friends and relatives who honor and celebrate my great-grandmother, Vi taqʷšəblu Hilbert. She guided me through this story.

Thank you to all the folks who let me crash on their couches while I was still looking for my permanent home, thanks to the friends who put our band up on tour, who gave us coffee in the morning and fed us. Thanks to the friends who still make me mix tapes and zines, who send me songs of the day. Thank you to my wild and beautiful partner Blaine for showing me love could be this way and for making me laugh even when I was really, *really* bummed out at points during this writing process.

And thank you to Tania, for that phone call in the fairgrounds and for the Dentalium. "We wear it to remember that we are loved."

Sasha taqʷšəblu LaPointe is a Coast Salish author from the Nooksack and Upper Skagit Indian tribes. She received a double MFA in creative nonfiction and poetry from the Institute of American Indian Arts. She lives in Tacoma, Washington. Find out more at sasha-lapointe.com.